Explore Your

Bible

Explore Your

Bible

199 Bible Topics with References

BARBOUR
PUBLISHING

© 2010 by Barbour Publishing, Inc.

ISBN 978-1-60260-833-7

Published by Barbour Publishing, Inc., P.O. Box 719,
Uhrichsville, Ohio 44683 www.barbourbooks.com

*Our mission is to publish and distribute inspirational products offering
exceptional value and biblical encouragement to the masses.*

 Member of the
Evangelical Christian
Publishers Association

Printed in the United States of America.

Contents

Introduction

When you want to find a key Bible topic fast, turn to *Explore Your Bible*—it provides nearly 2,500 references on 199 important subjects.

Bible concordances are valuable tools, but unless you know the exact word to search for, you might miss an important truth. With *Explore Your Bible*, you'll search by topic—from "Access to God" to "Fear, Unholy" to "Zeal." Each topic features several references, often with helpful subtopics.

Based on R. A. Torrey's classic *New Topical Textbook*, this handbook is useful for personal or group study. It encourages you to dig deeper into God's Word—and get more from it!

1. Access to God

Is of God. . .Ps. 65:4

Is by Christ. . .John 10:7, 9; 14:6; Rom. 5:1–2;
   Eph. 2:13; 3:10–12; Heb. 7:19–25; 10:19–22;
   1 Pet. 3:18

Is by the Holy Spirit. . .Eph. 2:18

Obtained through faith. . .Acts 14:27; Rom. 5:2;
   Eph. 3:12; Heb. 11:6

In prayer. . .Deut. 4:7; Matt. 6:6; 1 Pet. 1:17
   (*See also* Prayer)

In His temple. . .Ps. 15:1; 27:4; 43:3; 65:4

To obtain mercy and grace. . .Heb. 4:16

The wicked commanded to seek. . .Isa. 55:6; James 4:8

Urge others to seek. . .Isa. 2:3; Jer. 31:6

Promises connected with. . .Ps. 145:18; Isa. 55:3;
   Matt. 6:6; James 4:8

Blessedness of. . .Ps. 16:11; 65:4; 73:28

2. Adoption

Is by faith. . .Gal. 3:7, 26

Is of God's grace. . .Ezek. 16:3–6; Rom. 4:16–17;
   Eph. 1:5–6, 11

Is through Christ. . .John 1:8, 12; Gal. 4:4–5; Eph. 1:5;
   Heb. 2:9–10, 13

New birth connected with. . .John 1:12–13

The Holy Spirit is a witness of. . .Rom. 8:16

Being led by the Spirit is an evidence of. . .Rom. 8:14

Saints receive the spirit of. . .Rom. 8:15; Gal. 4:6

Subjects saints to the fatherly discipline of God. . .
   Deut. 8:5; 2 Sam. 7:14; Prov. 3:11–12; Heb. 12:5–11

God is long-suffering and merciful toward the
   partakers of. . .Jer. 31:1, 9, 20

Should lead to holiness. . .2 Cor. 6:17–18; 7:1;
   Phil. 2:15; 1 John 3:2–3

Safety of those who receive. . .Prov. 14:26

Entitles to an inheritance. . .Matt. 13:43; Rom. 8:17;
   Gal. 3:29; 4:7; Eph. 3:6

Is to be pleaded in prayer. . .Isa. 63:16; Matt. 6:9

3. Affections, The

Should be supremely set on God. . .Deut. 6:5;
   Mark 12:30

Should be set
   • Upon the commandments of God. . .
     Ps. 19:8–10; 119:20, 97, 103, 167
   • Upon the house and worship of God. . .
     1 Chron. 29:3; 26:8; 27:4; 84:1–2
   • Upon the people of God. . .Ps. 16:3; Rom. 12:10;
     2 Cor. 7:13–15; 1 Thess. 2:8

Should be zealously engaged for God. . .
   Ps. 69:9; 119:139; Gal. 4:18

Christ claims first place in. . .Matt. 10:37; Luke 14:26

Incited by communion with Christ. . .Luke 24:32

Blessedness of making God the object of. . .Ps. 91:14

Should not grow cold. . .Ps. 106:12–13; Matt. 24:12–13
   Gal. 4:15; Rev. 2:4–5

Of saints, supremely set on God. . .
   Ps. 42:1; 73:25; 119:10

Of the wicked, not sincerely set on God. . .Isa. 58:1–2;
   Ezek. 33:31–32; Luke 8:13

Carnal affections should be put to death. . .
   Rom. 8:13; 13:14; 1 Cor. 9:27; Col. 3:5; 1 Thess. 4:4–5

False teachers seek to captivate. . .Gal. 1:9–10; 4:17;
   2 Tim. 3:2, 6; 2 Pet. 2:3, 18; Rev. 2:14, 20

Of the wicked, are unnatural and perverted. . .
   Rom. 1:28–31; 2 Tim. 3:2–3; 2 Pet. 2:10

4. Afflictions

◇◇

God appoints. . .2 Kings 6:33; Job 5:6, 17; Ps. 66:10–11;
   Amos 3:6; Mic. 6:9

God dispenses, as He will. . .Job 11:10; Isa. 45:7

God regulates the measure of. . .Ps. 80:4–5; Isa. 9:1;
   Jer. 46:28

God determines, but does not willingly send. . .
   Lam. 3:25, 33

Man is born to. . .Job 5:6–7; 14:1

Saints appointed to. . .1 Thess. 3:2–3

Consequent to the fall. . .Gen. 3:16–19

Sin produces. . .Job 4:8; Prov. 1:31

Afflictions Made Beneficial

Always less than we deserve. . .Ezra 9:13; Ps. 103:10

Frequently terminate in good. . .Gen. 50:20;
   Exod. 1:11–12; Deut. 8:15–16; Jer. 24:5–6;
   Ezek. 20:36–37

Tempered with mercy. . .Ps. 78:38–39; 106:43–46;
   Isa. 30:18–21; Lam. 3:32; Mic. 7:7–9; Nah. 1:12

Afflicted Saints

Saints are to expect. . .John 16:33; Acts 14:22

Of saints, are comparatively light. . .Acts 20:23–24;
   Rom. 8:18; 2 Cor. 4:17

Of saints, are only temporary. . .Ps. 30:5; 103:9;
   Isa. 54:7–8; John 16:20; 1 Pet. 1:6; 5:10

Saints have joy under. . .Job 5:17; James 5:11

5. Ambition

God condemns. . .Gen. 11:1–7; Isa. 5:8

Christ condemns. . .
   Matt. 18:1, 3–4; 20:25–26; 23:11–12

Saints should avoid. . .Ps. 131:1–2

Vanity of. . .Job 20:5–9; 24:22, 24; Ps. 49:11–20

Leads to strife and contention. . .James 4:1–2

Punishment of. . .Prov. 17:19; Isa. 14:12–15;
   Ezek. 31:10–11; Obad. 3–4

Connected with
   • Pride. . .Hab. 2:5
   • Covetousness. . .Hab. 2:8–9

- Cruelty. . .Hab. 2:12

Exemplified

- Adam and Eve. . .Gen. 3:5–6
- Builders of Babel. . .Gen. 11:4, 8
- Sons of Zebedee. . .Matt. 20:20–21

6. Anger

<<<<<<<<<<<<<<<<<<<<<<<<<<<<<<<<<<<<<<<<<<<<<<<

Forbidden. . .Eccles. 7:9; Matt. 5:22; Rom. 12:19

A work of the flesh. . .Gal. 5:19–20

A characteristic of fools. . .

   Prov. 12:16; 14:29; 27:3; Eccles. 7:9

Connected with

- Pride. . .Prov. 21:24
- Cruelty. . .Gen. 49:7; Prov. 27:3–4
- Malice and blasphemy. . .Col. 3:8
- Strife and contention. . .
     Prov. 21:19; 29:22; 30:33

Brings its own punishment. . .Job 5:2;

   Prov. 19:19; 25:28

Grievous words stir up. . .Judg. 12:4; 2 Sam. 19:43;

   Prov. 15:1

Should not lead us into sin. . .Ps. 37:8; Eph. 4:26–27

In prayer, forbidden. . .1 Tim. 2:8

Children should not be provoked to. . .Eph. 6:4;

   Col. 3:21

Be slow to. . .Prov. 15:18; 16:32; 19:11; Titus 1:7;

   James 1:19

Avoid those given to. . .Gen. 49:6; Prov. 22:24

7. Anger of God, The

Averted by Christ. . .Luke 2:11, 14; Rom. 5:9;
2 Cor. 5:18–19; Eph. 2:13–14, 17; Col. 1:20;
1 Thess. 1:10

Is slow. . .Ps. 103:8; Isa. 48:9; Jon. 4:2; Nah. 1:3

Is righteous. . .Ps. 58:10–11; Lam. 1:18;
Rom. 2:6, 8; 3:5–6; Rev. 16:6–7

The justice of, not to be questioned. . .Rom. 9:18, 20, 22

Aggravated by continual provocation. . .Num. 32:13–14

Specially reserved for the day of wrath. . .Zeph. 1:14–18;
Matt. 25:41; Rom. 2:5, 8; 2 Thess. 1:8;
Rev. 6:17; 11:18; 19:15

Against
- The wicked. . .Ps. 7:11; 21:8–9; Isa. 3:8;13:9;
Nah. 1:2–3; Rom. 1:18; 2:8; Eph. 5:6; Col. 3:6
- Those who forsake Him. . .Ezra 8:22; Isa. 1:4
- Idolatry. . .Deut. 29:17, 20, 27–28; 32:19–22;
Josh. 23:16; 2 Kings 22:17; Ps. 78:58–59;
Jer. 44:3
- Sin, in saints. . .
Ps. 89:30–32; 90:7–9; 99:8; 102:9–10; Isa. 47:6

Extreme, against those who oppose the gospel. . .
Ps. 2:2–3, 5; 1 Thess. 2:16

Tempered with mercy to saints. . .Ps. 30:5;
Isa. 26:20; 54:8; 57:15–16; Jer. 30:11; Mic. 7:9–11

To be borne with submission. . .2 Sam. 24:17;
Lam. 3:39, 43; Mic. 7:9

Should lead to repentance. . .Isa. 42:24–25; Jer. 4:8

8. Anointing of the Holy Spirit

Is from God. . .2 Cor. 1:21

That Christ should receive

- Foretold. . .Ps. 45:7; Isa. 61:1; Dan. 9:24
- Fulfilled. . .Luke 4:18, 21; Acts 4:27; 10:38; Heb. 1:8–9

God preserves those who receive. . .Ps. 18:50; 20:6; 89:20–23

Saints receive. . .Isa. 61:1, 3; 1 John 2:20

Abides in saints. . .1 John 2:27

Guides into all truth. . .1 John 2:27

Typified. . .Exod. 40:13–15; Lev. 8:12; 1 Sam. 16:13; 1 Kings 19:16

9. Antichrist

Denies the Father and the Son. . .1 John 2:22

Denies the incarnation of Christ. . .1 John 4:3; 2 John 1:7

Spirit of, prevalent in apostolic times. . .1 John 2:18

Deceit, a characteristic of. . .2 John 1:7

10. Ascension of Christ, The

Prophecies about. . .Ps. 24:7; 68:18; Eph. 4:7–8

Foretold by Jesus Himself. . .
   John 6:61–62; 7:33; 14:23–28; 16:5,19; 20:17

Forty days after Jesus' resurrection. . .Acts 1:3

Described. . .Acts 1:9

From Mount Olivet. . .Luke 24:50–51; Acts 1:12

While blessing His disciples. . .Luke 24:50–51

When He had atoned for sin. . .Heb. 9:11–12; 10:12

Was triumphant. . .Ps. 68:18

Was to supreme power and dignity. . .Luke 24:26;
   Eph. 1:20–21; 1 Pet. 3:22

To intercede. . .Rom. 8:34; Heb. 9:24

To send the Holy Spirit. . .John 16:7; Acts 2:33

To receive gifts for men. . .Ps. 68:18; Eph. 4:8, 11

To prepare a place for His people. . .John 14:2

His second coming will be similar. . .Acts 1:10–11

11. Assurance

Produced by faith. . .Eph. 3:12; 2 Tim. 1:12;
   Heb. 10:22

Made full by hope. . .Heb. 6:11, 19

Confirmed by love. . .1 John 3:14, 19; 4:18

Is the effect of righteousness. . .Isa. 32:17

Saints privileged to have, of

• Their election. . .Ps. 4:3; 1 Thess. 1:4

- Their redemption. . .Job 19:25
- Their adoption. . .Rom. 8:16; 1 John 3:2
- Their salvation. . .Isa. 12:2
- Eternal life. . .1 John 5:13
- The unalienable love of God. . .Rom. 8:38–39
- Union with God and Christ. . .1 Cor. 6:15;
  2 Cor. 13:5; Eph. 5:29–30; 1 John 2:5; 4:13
- Peace with God by Christ. . .Rom. 5:1
- Answers to prayer. . .1 John 3:22; 5:14–15
- Comfort in affliction. . .Ps. 73:26; Luke 4:18–19;
  2 Cor. 4:8–10, 16–17
- Support in death. . .Ps. 23:4
- A glorious resurrection. . .Job 19:26; Ps. 17:15;
  Phil. 3:21; 1 John 3:2
- A crown. . .2 Tim. 4:7–8; James 1:12

12. Atonement

Explained. . .Rom. 5:8–11; 2 Cor. 5:18–19; Gal. 1:4;
  1 John 2:2; 4:10
Foretold. . .Isa. 53:4–6, 8–12; Dan. 9:24–27;
  Zech. 13:1, 7; John 11:50–51
Effected by Christ alone. . .John 1:29, 36; Acts 4:10, 12;
  1 Thess. 1:10; 1 Tim. 2:5–6; Heb. 2:9; 1 Pet. 2:24
Was voluntary. . .Ps. 40:6–8; Heb. 10:5–9;
  John 10:11, 15, 17–18
Saints praise God for. . .Rev. 5:9–13
Commemorated in the Lord's Supper. . .Matt. 26:26–28;
  1 Cor. 11:23–26

Day of Atonement

Tenth day of seventh month. . .Lev. 23:26–27

A day of humiliation. . .Lev. 16:29, 31; 23:27

Observed as a Sabbath. . .Lev. 23:28, 32

Offerings to be made on. . .Lev. 16:3, 5–15

Atonement Under the Law

Made by sacrifice. . .Lev. 1:4–5

By priests alone. . .1 Chron. 6:49; 2 Chron. 29:24

13. Backsliding

Is turning from God. . .1 Kings 11:9

Is leaving the first love. . .Rev. 2:4

Is departing from the simplicity of the gospel. . .
 2 Cor. 11:3; Gal. 3:1–3; 5:4, 7

God is displeased at. . .Ps. 78:57, 59

Warnings against. . .Ps. 85:8; 1 Cor. 10:12

Guilt and consequences of. . .Num. 14:43; Ps. 125:5;
 Isa. 59:2, 9–11; Jer. 5:6; 8:5, 13; 15:6; Luke 9:62

Brings its own punishment. . .Prov. 14:14; Jer. 2:19

A haughty spirit leads to. . .Prov. 16:18

Pray to be restored from. . .Ps. 80:3; 85:4; Lam. 5:21

Punishment of tempting others to the sin of. . .
 Prov. 28:10; Matt. 18:6

Not hopeless. . .Ps. 37:24; Prov. 24:16

Endeavor to bring back those guilty of. . .Gal. 6:1;
 James 5:19–20

Sin of, to be confessed. . .Isa. 59:12–14;
   Jer. 3:13–14; 14:7–9
Pardon of, promised. . .2 Chron. 7:14;
   Jer. 3:12; 31:20; 36:3
Healing of, promised. . Jer. 3:22; Hosea 14:4
Blessedness of those who keep from. . .Prov. 28:14;
   Isa. 26:3–4; Col. 1:21–23

14. Baptism

Sanctioned by Christ's submission to it. . .Matt. 3:13–15;
   Luke 3:21
Adopted by Christ. . John 3:22; 4:1–2
Appointed an ordinance of the Christian church. . .
   Matt. 28:19–20; Mark 16:15–16
To be administered in the name of the Father, Son,
   and Holy Spirit. . .Matt. 28:19
Water, the outward and visible sign in. . .
   Acts 8:36; 10:47
Regeneration, the inward and spiritual grace of. . .
   John 3:3, 5–6; Rom. 6:3–4, 11
Remission of sins, signified by. . .Acts 2:38; 22:16
Confession of sin necessary to. . .Matt. 3:6
Repentance necessary to. . .Acts 2:38
Faith necessary to. . .Acts 8:36–37; 18:8

Baptism with the Holy Spirit
Foretold. . .Ezek. 36:25
Is through Christ. . .Titus 3:5–6
Promised to saints. . .Acts 1:5; 2:38–39; 11:16
Renews and cleanses the soul. . .Titus 3:5; 1 Pet. 3:20–21
The Word of God instrumental to. . .Acts 10:44;
  Eph. 5:26

15. Blasphemy

Christ assailed with. . .Matt. 10:25; Luke 22:63–65;
  1 Pet. 4:13–14
Charged upon Christ. . .Matt. 9:2–3; 26:64–65;
  John 10:33, 36
Charged upon saints. . .Acts 6:11, 13
Proceeds from the heart. . .Matt. 15:19
Forbidden. . .Exod. 20:7; Col. 3:8
The wicked addicted to. . .Ps. 74:18; Isa. 52:5;
  2 Tim. 3:2; Rev.16:11, 21
Idolatry counted as. . .Isa. 65:7; Ezek. 20:27–28
Hypocrisy counted as. . .Rev. 2:9
Give no occasion for. . .2 Sam. 12:14; 1 Tim. 6:1
Against the Holy Spirit, unpardonable. . .Matt. 12:31–32
Connected with folly and pride. . .2 Kings 19:22;
  Ps. 74:18
Punishment of. . .Lev. 24:16; Isa. 65:7;
  Ezek. 20:27–33; 35:11–12

16. Blessed, The

Whom God calls. . .Isa. 51:2; Rev. 19:9

Whose sins are forgiven. . .Ps. 32:1–2; Rom. 4:7

Whom God disciplines. . .Job 5:17; Ps. 94:12

Who suffer for Christ. . .Luke 6:22

Who trust in God. . .Ps. 2:12; 34:8; 40:4; 84:12;
    Jer. 17:7

Who hear and keep the Word of God. . .Ps. 119:2;
    James 1:25; Matt. 13:16; Luke 11:28; Rev. 1:3; 22:7

Who delight in the commandments of God. . .Ps. 112:1

Whose strength is in the Lord. . .Ps. 84:5

Who endure temptation. . .James 1:12

The pure in heart. . .Matt. 5:8

The faithful. . .Prov. 28:20

The meek. . .Matt. 5:5

The merciful. . .Matt. 5:7

The peacemakers. . .Matt. 5:9

17. Blindness, Spiritual

The effect of sin. . .Isa. 29:9–10; Matt. 6:23;
    John 3:19–20

A work of the devil. . .2 Cor. 4:4

Leads to all evil. . .Eph. 4:17–19

Of ministers, fatal to themselves and to the people. . .
    Matt. 15:14

The wicked are in. . .Ps. 82:2, 5; Jer. 5:21

Pray for the removal of. . .Ps. 13:3; 119:18

Christ appointed to remove. . .Isa. 42:6–7; Luke 4:18;
    John 8:12; 9:39; 2 Cor. 4:6

Christ's ministers are lights to remove. . .Matt. 5:14;
  Acts 26:16–18

Saints are delivered from. . .John 8:12; Eph. 5:8;
  Col. 1:13; 1 Thess. 5:4–5; 1 Pet. 2:9

18. Blood

The life of animals. . .Gen. 9:4; Lev. 17:11, 14

Of all men the same. . .Acts 17:26

Eating of, forbidden to

- Man after the flood. . .Gen. 9:4
- The Israelites under the law. . .Lev. 3:17; 17:10, 12
- The early Christians. . .Acts 15:20, 29

Shedding of human

- Forbidden. . .Gen. 9:5
- Hateful to God. . .Prov. 6:16–17
- Defiling to the land. . .Ps. 106:38
- Defiling to the person. . .Isa. 59:3
- Always punished. . .Gen. 9:6

Of legal sacrifices

- For atonement. . .Exod. 30:10; Lev. 17:11
- For purification. . .Heb. 9:13, 19–22

Waters of Egypt turned into, as a judgment. . .
  Exod. 7:17–21

19. Bondage, Spiritual

Is to the devil. . .1 Tim. 3:7; 2 Tim. 2:26

Is to the fear of death. . .Heb. 2:14–15

Is to sin. . .John 8:34; Acts 8:23; Rom. 6:16; 7:23;
    Gal. 4:3; 2 Pet. 2:19

Deliverance from, promised. . .Isa. 42:6–7

Christ delivers from. . .Luke 4:18, 21; John 8:36;
    Rom. 7:24–25; Eph. 4:7–8

The gospel, the instrument of deliverance from. . .
    John 8:32; Rom. 8:2

Saints are delivered from. . .Rom. 6:18, 22

Deliverance from, illustrated. . .Deut. 4:20

Typified, by Israel in Egypt. . .Exod. 1:13–14

20. Call of God, The

By Christ. . .Isa. 55:4–5; Rom. 1:6

By His Spirit. . .Rev. 22:17

By His works. . .Ps. 19:1–3; Rom. 1:20

By His ministers. . .Jer. 35:15; 2 Cor. 5:20

By His gospel. . .2 Thess. 2:14

Is from darkness. . .1 Pet. 2:9

Addressed to all. . .Isa. 45:22; Matt. 20:16

Most reject. . .Prov. 1:24; Matt. 20:16

Effectual to saints. . .Ps. 110:3; Acts 2:47; 13:48;
    1 Cor. 1:24

To man is
- Of grace. . .Gal. 1:15; 2 Tim. 1:9
- According to the purpose of God. . .Rom. 8:28;
  9:11, 23–24

Walk worthy of. . .Eph. 4:1

Blessedness of receiving. . .Rev. 19:9

Praise God for. . .1 Pet. 2:9

21. Care, Overmuch

About earthly things, forbidden. . .Matt. 6:25;
  Luke 12:22, 29; John 6:27

God's providential goodness should keep us from. . .
  Matt. 6:26, 28, 30; Luke 22:35

God's promises should keep us from. . .Heb. 13:5

Trust in God should free us from. . .Jer. 17:7–8;
  Dan. 3:16–18

Should be cast on God. . .Ps. 37:5; 55:22; Prov. 16:3;
  1 Pet. 5:7

An obstruction to the gospel. . .Matt. 13:22;
  Luke 8:14; 14:18–20

Be without. . .1 Cor. 7:32; Phil. 4:6

Unbecoming in saints. . .2 Tim. 2:4

Uselessness of. . .Matt. 6:27; Luke 12:25–26

Vanity of. . .Ps. 39:6; Eccles. 4:8

Warning against. . .Luke 21:34

Sent as a punishment to the wicked. . .Ezek. 4:16; 12:19

22. Character, of Saints

Bold. . .Prov. 28:1; Rom. 13:3

Contrite. . .Isa. 57:15; 66:2

Devout. . .Acts 8:2; 22:12

Faithful. . .Rev. 17:14

Fearing God. . .Acts 10:2

Following Christ. . .John 10:4, 27

Humble. . .Ps. 34:2; 1 Pet. 5:5

Obedient. . .Rom. 16:19; 1 Pet. 1:14

Character of the Wicked

Blasphemous. . .Luke 22:63–65; Rev. 16:9

Covetous. . .Mic. 2:2; Rom. 1:29

Deceitful. . .Ps. 5:6; Rom. 3:13

Destructive. . .Isa. 59:7

Disobedient. . .Neh. 9:26; Titus 3:3; 1 Pet. 2:7

Foolish. . .Deut. 32:6; Ps. 5:5

Ungodly. . .Prov. 16:27

23. Charity

Explained. . .1 Cor. 13:4–7

Enjoined. . .Col. 3:14 (*See also* Love to Man)

24. Chastity

Commanded. . .Exod. 20:14; Prov. 31:3; Acts 15:20;
Rom. 13:13; Col. 3:5; 1 Thess. 4:3

Required in use of eyes. . .Job 31:1; Matt. 5:28

Required in heart. . .Prov. 6:25

Required in speech. . .Eph. 5:3

Keep the body in. . .1 Cor. 6:13, 15–18

Preserved by wisdom. . .Prov. 2:10–11, 16; 7:1–5

Saints are kept in. . .Eccles. 7:26

Advantages of. . .1 Pet. 3:1–2

Shun those devoid of. . .1 Cor. 5:11; 1 Pet. 4:3

Drunkenness destructive to. . .Prov. 23:31–33

Motives for. . .1 Cor. 6:19; 1 Thess. 4:7

25. Children, Good

Christ was an example to. . .Luke 2:51; John 19:26–27

Are a gift from God. . .Gen. 33:5; Ps. 127:3

Should be

- Brought to Christ. . .Mark 10:13–16
- Brought early to the house of God. . .1 Sam. 1:24
- Instructed in the ways of God. . .Deut. 31:12–13;
  Prov. 22:6

Should

- Obey God. . .Deut. 30:2
- Fear God. . .Prov. 24:21
- Remember God. . .Eccles. 12:1

- Attend to parental teaching. . .Prov. 1:8–9
- Honor parents. . .Exod. 20:12; Heb. 12:9
- Obey parents. . .Prov. 6:20; Eph. 6:1

An heritage from the Lord. . .Ps. 113:9; 127:3
Know the scriptures. . .2 Tim. 3:15
Shall be blessed. . .Prov. 3:1–4; Eph. 6:2–3

Children, Wicked
Know not God. . .1 Sam. 2:12
Are void of understanding. . .Prov. 7:7
Are proud. . .Isa. 3:5

26. Christ

Character of Christ
Altogether lovely. . .Song of Sol. 5:16
Holy. . .Luke 1:35; Acts 4:27; Rev. 3:7
Righteous. . .Isa. 53:10–11; Heb. 1:8–9
Good. . .Matt. 19:14, 16
Faithful. . .Isa. 11:1–2, 5; 1 Thess. 5:23–24
True. . .John 1:14; 7:16–18; 1 John 5:20
Just. . .Zech. 9:9; John 5:30; Acts 22:14
Patient. . .Isa. 53:4, 7; Matt. 27:1, 14

Christ Is God
As God over all. . .Ps. 45:6–7; Rom. 9:5
As the true God. . .Jer. 10:10; 1 John 5:20
As Son of God. . .Matt. 26:63–67
Appointed by God. . .Eph. 1:3, 18–22

Christ the King
On His throne. . .Zech. 6:12–13
Has an everlasting kingdom. . .Dan. 2:44; 7:13–14;
 Luke 1:32–33

Christ the Mediator
The only one between God and man. . .1 Tim. 2:5

Christ the Prophet
Foretold. . .Deut. 18:15, 18; Isa. 52:6–7; Nah. 1:15
Mighty in deed and word. . .Matt. 13:53–54;
 Mark 1:25, 27; Luke 4:14, 32; John 7:37–39, 46

Christ the Shepherd
His sheep
- He knows. . .John 10:7, 14, 27
- He calls. . .John 10:3, 6
- He laid down His life for. . .Zech. 13:7;
 Matt. 26:31; John 10:11, 15; Acts 20:28

27. Church, The
<><><><><><><><><><><><><><><><><><><><><><><><><>

Belongs to God. . .1 Tim. 3:15
The body of Christ. . .Eph. 1:22–23; Col. 1:24
Christ, the head of. . .Eph. 1:20–22; 5:23
Loved by Christ. . .Song of Sol. 7:10; Eph. 5:25
Purchased by the blood of Christ. . .Acts 20:28;
 Eph. 5:25; Heb. 9:12

Sanctified and cleansed by Christ. . .1 Cor. 6:11;
  Eph. 5:25–27
Subject to Christ. . .Rom. 7:4; Eph. 5:24
Shows forth the praises of God. . .Isa. 60:6
Clothed in righteousness. . .Rev. 19:8
Unity of. . .Rom. 12:5; 1 Cor. 10:17; 12:12; Gal. 3:28
Is edified by the Word. . .1 Cor. 14:4, 13; Eph. 4:15–16

28. Commandments, The Ten

◇◇◇◇◇◇◇◇◇◇◇◇◇◇◇◇◇◇◇◇◇◇◇◇◇◇◇◇◇◇◇◇◇◇◇◇

Spoken by God. . .Exod. 20:1–17; Deut. 5:4–22
Written by God. . .Exod. 32:15–16; 34:1, 28;
  Deut. 4:12–13; 10:1, 4
Enumerated. . .Exod. 20:3–17
Summarized by Christ. . .Matt. 22:35–40
Law of, is spiritual. . .Matt. 5:28; Rom. 7:14
  (*See also* Law of God)

29. Commerce

◇◇◇◇◇◇◇◇◇◇◇◇◇◇◇◇◇◇◇◇◇◇◇◇◇◇◇◇◇◇◇◇◇◇◇◇

The barter of one commodity for another. . .
  1 Kings 5:8, 11
The exchange of commodities for money. . .
  1 Kings 10:28–29
Called
  • Trade. . .Gen. 34:10; Matt. 25:16
  • Traffic. . .Gen. 42:34; Ezek. 17:4

- Buying and selling. . .James 4:13

Inland, by caravans. . .Isa. 21:13

Maritime, by ships. . .2 Chron. 8:18; 9:21

Persons of distinction engaged in. . .Isa. 23:8

Increased the wealth of nations and individuals. . .
   2 Chron. 9:20–22; Prov. 31:14–18; Ezek. 28:4–5

Articles of
- Gold. . .2 Chron. 8:18
- Oil. . .1 Kings 5:11; Ezek. 27:17
- Precious stones. . .Ezek. 27:16, 22; 28:13, 16

30. Communion

◇◇◇◇◇◇◇◇◇◇◇◇◇◇◇◇◇◇◇◇◇◇◇◇◇◇◇◇◇◇◇◇◇

Communion of Saints

Christ is present in. . .Matt. 18:20

In the Lord's Supper. . .1 Cor. 10:17

In holy conversation. . .Mal. 3:16

In prayer for each other. . .2 Cor. 1:11; Eph. 6:18

Delight of. . .Ps. 16:3; 42:4; 133:1–3; Rom. 15:32

Communion of the Lord's Supper

Is the communion of the body and blood of Christ. . .
   1 Cor. 10:16

Self-examination commanded before taking part. . .
   1 Cor. 11:28, 31

Newness of heart and life necessary to worthy
   participation. . .1 Cor. 5:7–8

Partakers of, be wholly separate to God. . .1 Cor. 10:21

Communion with God

Reconciliation must precede. . .Amos 3:3

Holiness essential to. . .2 Cor. 6:14–16

Promised to the obedient. . .John 14:23

31. *Condemnation*

The sentence of God against sin. . .Matt. 25:41

Universal, caused by the offense of Adam. . .
    Rom. 5:12, 16, 18

Inseparable consequence of sin. . .Prov. 12:2;
    Rom. 6:23

Increased by

- Unbelief. . .John 3:18–19
- Pride. . .1 Tim. 3:6
- Hypocrisy. . .Matt. 23:14

Saints are delivered from, by Christ. . .John 3:18; 5:24;
    Rom. 8:1, 33–34

Of the wicked, an example. . .2 Pet. 2:6–7; Jude 7

Chastisements are designed to rescue us from. . .
    Ps. 94:12–13; 1 Cor. 11:32

Unbelievers remain under. . .John 3:18, 36

32. Conduct, Christian

Believing God. . .Mark 11:22; John 14:11–12

Fearing God. . .Eccles. 12:13; 1 Pet. 2:17

Loving God. . .Deut. 6:5; Matt. 22:37

Following God. . .Eph. 5:1; 1 Pet. 1:15–16

Obeying God. . .Luke 1:6; 1 John 5:3

Loving one another. . .John 15:12; Rom. 12:10;
    1 Cor. 13:1–13; Eph. 5:2; Heb. 13:1

Striving for the faith. . .Phil. 1:27; Jude 3

Putting away all sin. . .1 Cor. 5:7; Heb. 12:1

Abstaining from all appearance of evil. . .1 Thess. 5:22

Perfecting holiness. . .Matt. 5:48; 2 Cor. 7:1;
    2 Tim. 3:17

Following after that which is good. . .Phil. 4:8;
    1 Thess. 5:15; 1 Tim. 6:11

Subduing the temper. . .Eph. 4:26; James 1:19

Honoring others. . .Ps. 15:4; Rom. 12:10

33. Confession

Confession of Christ

An evidence of union with God. . .1 John 4:15

Necessary to salvation. . .Rom. 10:9–10

Ensures His confessing us. . .Matt. 10:32

Persecution should not prevent us from. . .Mark 8:35;
    2 Tim. 2:12

Consequences of not confessing. . .Matt. 10:33

Confession of Sin

God requires. . .Lev. 5:5; Hosea 5:15

God regards. . .Job 33:27–28; Dan. 9:20–23

Promises to. . .Lev. 26:40–42; Prov. 28:13

Should be accompanied with

- Submission to punishment. . .Lev. 26:41;
  Neh. 9:33; Ezra 9:13
- Prayer for forgiveness. . .2 Sam. 24:10;
  Ps. 25:11; 51:1; Jer. 14:7–9, 20
- Forsaking sin. . .Prov. 28:13

Should be full and unreserved. . .Ps. 32:5; 51:3; 106:6

Followed by pardon. . .Ps. 32:5; 1 John 1:9

34. *Conscience*

Witnesses in man. . .Prov. 20:27; Rom. 2:15

Accuses of sin. . .Gen. 42:21; 2 Sam. 24:10; Matt. 27:3;
Acts 2:37

We should have the approval of. . .Job 27:6; Acts 24:16;
Rom. 9:1; 14:22

The blood of Christ alone can purify. . .
Heb. 9:14; 10:2–10, 22

Keep the faith in purity of. . .1 Tim. 1:19; 3:9

Of saints, pure and good. . .Heb. 13:18; 1 Pet. 3:16, 21

Submit to authority for. . .Rom. 13:5

Suffer patiently for. . .1 Pet. 2:19

Testimony of, a source of joy. . .2 Cor. 1:12; 1 John 3:21

Of others, not to be offended. . .Rom. 14:21;
1 Cor. 10:28–32

Of the wicked, defiled. . .Titus 1:15

Without spiritual illumination, a false guide. . .
  Acts 23:1; 26:9

35. Contentment

◇◇

With godliness is great gain. . .Ps. 37:16; 1 Tim. 6:6

Saints should exhibit
  • In their respective callings. . .1 Cor. 7:20
  • With appointed wages. . .Luke 3:14
  • With what things they have. . .Heb. 13:5
  • With food and clothing. . .1 Tim. 6:8

God's promises should lead to. . .Heb. 13:5

The wicked want. . .Isa. 5:8; Eccles. 5:10

Exemplified
  • David. . .Ps. 16:6
  • Paul. . .Phil. 4:11–12

36. Covenant, The

◇◇

Christ, the substance of. . .Isa. 42:6; 49:8

Christ, the Mediator of. . .Heb. 8:6; 9:15; 12:24

Christ, the Messenger of. . .Mal. 3:1

Renewed under the gospel. . .Jer. 31:31–33; Rom. 11:27;
  Heb. 8:8–10, 13

Is a covenant of peace. . .Isa. 54:9–10; Ezek. 34:25; 37:26

Is unalterable. . .Ps. 89:34; Isa. 54:10; 59:21; Gal. 3:17

Is everlasting. . .Ps. 111:9; Isa. 55:3; 61:8; Ezek. 16:60–63; Heb. 13:20

Blessings connected with. . .Isa. 56:4–7; Heb. 8:10–12

God is faithful to. . .Deut. 7:9; 1 Kings 8:23; Neh. 1:5; Dan. 9:4

God is ever mindful of. . .Ps. 105:8; 111:5; Luke 1:72

37. Covetousness

◇◇◇◇◇◇◇◇◇◇◇◇◇◇◇◇◇◇◇◇◇◇◇◇◇◇◇◇◇◇◇◇◇◇◇◇

Comes from the heart. . .Mark 7:22–23

Engrosses the heart. . .Ezek. 33:31; 2 Pet. 2:14

Is idolatry. . .Eph. 5:5; Col. 3:5

Is the root of all evil. . .1 Tim. 6:10

Is never satisfied. . .Eccles. 5:10; Hab. 2:5

Abhorred by God. . .Ps. 10:3

Forbidden. . .Exod. 20:17

Punishment of. . .Job 20:15; Isa. 57:17; Jer. 22:17–19; Mic. 2:2–3

Pray against. . .Ps. 119:36

Reward of those who hate. . .Prov. 28:16

Shall abound in the last days. . .2 Tim. 3:2; 2 Pet. 2:1–3

38. Creation

◇◇

The formation of things which had no previous existence. . .Rom. 4:17; Heb. 11:3

Effected

- By God. . .Gen. 1:1; 2:4–5
- In the beginning. . .Gen. 1:1; Matt. 24:21
- In six normal days. . .Exod. 20:11; 31:17
- According to God's purpose. . .Ps. 135:6
- For God's pleasure. . .Prov. 16:4; Rev. 4:11

By faith we believe, to be God's work. . .Heb. 11:3

Order of

- First day, making light and dividing it from darkness. . .Gen. 1:3–5; 2 Cor. 4:6
- Second day, making the firmament or atmosphere, and separating the waters. . . Gen. 1:6–8
- Third day, separating the land from the water, and making it fruitful. . .Gen. 1:9–13
- Fourth day, placing the sun, moon, and stars to give light. . .Gen. 1:14–19
- Fifth day, making birds, insects, and fishes. . . Gen. 1:20–23
- Sixth day, making beasts of the earth, and man. . . Gen. 1:24, 28

God rested from, on the seventh day. . .Gen. 2:2–3

A subject of joy to angels. . .Job 38:4, 7

39. Creditors

Might demand

- Pledges. . .Deut. 24:10–11; Prov. 22:27
- Security of others. . .Prov. 6:1; 22:26
- Mortgages on property. . .Neh. 5:3
- Bills or promissory notes. . .Luke 16:6–7

Prohibited from

- Taking millstones in pledge. . .Deut. 24:6
- Violently selecting pledges. . .Deut. 24:10
- Demanding interest from brethren. . .
  Exod. 22:25; Lev. 25:36–37
- Demanding debts from brethren during
  sabbatical year. . .Deut. 15:1–3

Sometimes entirely released debts. . .Neh. 5:10–12;
  Matt. 18:27; Luke 7:42

Often cruel in exacting debts. . .Neh. 5:7–9;
  Job 24:3–9; Matt. 18:28–30

Often exacted debts

- By selling the debtor or taking him for a servant. . .
  Matt. 18:25; Exod. 21:2
- By selling the debtor's property. . .Matt. 18:25
- By selling the debtor's family. . .2 Kings 4:1;
  Job 24:9; Matt. 18:25
- By imprisonment. . .Matt. 5:25–26; 18:34

40. Death

Death, Eternal

The necessary consequence of sin. . .
    Rom. 6:16, 21; 8:13; James 1:15

Christ, the only way of escape from. . .John 3:16; 8:51;
    Acts 4:10–12

Saints shall escape. . .Rev. 2:11; 20:6

Conquered by Christ. . .Rom. 6:9; Rev. 1:18

Death, Natural

Christ delivers from the fear of. . .Heb. 2:13, 15

Pray to be prepared for. . .Ps. 39:4, 13; 90:12

Death of Christ, The

Acceptable, as a sacrifice to God. . .Matt. 20:28;
    Eph. 5:2; 1 Thess. 5:10

Was voluntary. . .Isa. 53:12; Matt. 26:53;
    John 10:17–18

Was undeserved. . .Isa. 53:9

Death of Saints, The

Asleep in Christ. . .1 Cor. 15:18; 1 Thess. 4:14

Is blessed. . .Rev. 14:13

Is gain. . .Phil. 1:21

Precious in God's sight. . .Ps. 116:15

God is with them in. . .Ps. 23:4

Death of the Wicked, The

God has no pleasure in. . .Ezek. 18:23, 32

Death, Spiritual

Alienation from God is. . .Eph. 4:18
Unbelief is. . .John 3:36; 1 John 5:12
Is a consequence of the fall. . .Rom. 5:15

41. Decision

Necessary to the service of God. . .Luke 9:62
Exhibited in

- Seeking God with the heart. . .2 Chron. 15:12
- Keeping the commandments of God. . .Neh. 10:29
- Being on the Lord's side. . .Exod. 32:26
- Following God fully. . .Num. 14:24; 32:12; Josh. 14:8
- Serving God. . .Isa. 56:6
- Loving God perfectly. . .Deut. 6:5
- Blessedness of. . .Josh. 1:7

Opposed to

- A divided service. . .Matt. 6:24
- Double-mindedness. . .James 1:8
- Halting between two opinions. . .1 Kings 18:21
- Turning to the right or left. . .Deut. 5:32
- Not setting the heart aright. . .Ps. 78:8, 37

42. Dedication

Consecration of a place of worship. . .2 Chron. 2:4

Solemn confirmation of a covenant. . .Heb. 9:18

Devoting anything to sacred uses. . .1 Chron. 28:12

Subjects of
- Tabernacle. . .Num. 7:1–89
- Persons. . .Exod. 22:29; 1 Sam. 1:11
- Property. . .Lev. 27:28; Matt. 15:5
- Houses when built. . .Deut. 20:5

Things dedicated to God
- Esteemed holy. . .Lev. 27:28; 2 Kings 12:18
- Placed with the treasures of the Lord's house. . .
  1 Kings 7:51; 2 Chron. 5:1

Illustration of devotedness to God. . .Ps. 119:38

43. Defilement

Forbidden to the Jews. . .Lev. 11:44–45

Causes of, improperly enlarged by tradition. . .Mark 7:2;
  Matt. 15:20

Moral, caused by
- Following the sins of the heathen. . .Lev. 18:24
- Seeking after wizards. . .Lev. 19:31
- Making and serving idols. . .
  Ezek. 20:17–18; 22:3–4; 23:7
- Blood-shedding. . .Isa. 59:3

Moral, punished. . .Lev. 18:24–25, 28–29

Cleansed by legal offerings. . .Num. 19:18–19; Heb. 9:13

Neglecting purification from, punished by cutting off. . .
Num. 19:13, 20

Ceremonial, abolished under the gospel. . .Acts 10:15;
Rom. 14:14; Col. 2:20–22

44. Delighting in God

Commanded. . .Ps. 37:4

Reconciliation leads to. . .Job 22:21, 26

Observing the Sabbath leads to. . .Isa. 58:13–14

Saints' experience in

- Communion with God. . .Song of Sol. 2:3
- The law of God. . .Ps. 1:1; 119:24, 35
- The goodness of God. . .Neh. 9:25
- The comforts of God. . .Ps. 94:19

Hypocrites

- Pretend to. . .Isa. 58:2
- In heart despise. . .Job 27:8, 10; Jer. 6:8, 10

Promises for. . .Ps. 37:4

Blessedness. . .Ps. 112:1

45. Denial of Christ

In doctrine. . .Mark 8:38; 2 Tim. 1:8

In practice. . .Phil. 3:8, 10; Titus 1:16

A characteristic of false teachers. . .2 Pet. 2:1; Jude 4

Is the spirit of Antichrist. . .1 John 2:22–23; 4:3

Christ will deny those guilty of. . .Matt. 10:33;
    2 Tim. 2:12

Leads to destruction. . .2 Pet. 2:1; Jude 4, 14–15

Exemplified

- Peter. . .Matt. 26:69–75
- The Jews. . .John 18:28–40; Acts 3:13–14

46. Despair

Produced in the wicked by divine judgments. . .
    Deut. 28:34, 65–67; Rev. 9:4, 6; 16:10

Leads to

- Continuing in sin. . .Jer. 2:25; 18:12
- Blasphemy. . .Isa. 8:21; Rev. 16:10–11

Shall seize upon the wicked at the appearing of Christ. . .
    Rev. 6:16

Saints sometimes tempted to. . .Job 7:6; Lam. 3:18

Saints enabled to overcome. . .2 Cor. 4:8–9

Trust in God, a preservative against. . .Ps. 42:5, 11

Exemplified

- Cain. . .Gen. 4:13–14
- Ahithophel. . .2 Sam. 17:23
- Judas. . .Matt. 27:5

47. Devil, The

Sinned against God. . .2 Pet. 2:4; 1 John 3:8

Cast out of heaven. . .Luke 10:18

Cast down to hell. . .2 Pet. 2:4; Jude 6

The author of the fall. . .Gen. 3:1, 6, 14, 24

Perverts the scripture. . .Matt. 4:6

Opposes God's work. . .Zech. 3:1; 1 Thess. 2:18

Hinders the gospel. . .Matt. 13:19; 2 Cor. 4:4

Works lying wonders. . .2 Thess. 2:9; Rev. 16:14

Assumes the form of an angel of light. . .2 Cor. 11:14

Saints

- Afflicted by, only as God permits. . .
  Job 1:12; 2:4–7
- Tempted by. . .1 Chron. 21:1; 1 Thess. 3:5
- Should resist. . .James 4:7; 1 Pet. 5:8–9
- Should be armed against. . .Eph. 6:11–16
- Should be watchful against. . .2 Cor. 2:11
- Shall finally triumph over. . .Rom. 16:20

Everlasting fire is prepared for. . .Matt. 25:41

Triumph over, by Christ

- In destroying the works of. . .1 John 3:8
- Completed by His death. . .Col. 2:14–15;
  Heb. 2:14

48. Diligence

Christ, an example. . .Mark 1:35; Luke 2:43–49
Required by God in
- Seeking Him. . .1 Chron. 22:19; Heb. 11:6
- Obeying Him. . .Deut. 6:17; 11:13
- Keeping the heart. . .Prov. 4:23
- Labors of love. . .Heb. 6:10–12
- Self-examination. . .Ps. 77:6
- Lawful business. . .Prov. 27:23; Eccles. 9:10
- Teaching religion. . .2 Tim. 4:2; Jude 3
- Instructing children. . .Deut. 11:19

Saints should abound in. . .2 Cor. 8:7
In the service of God
- Is not in vain. . .1 Cor. 15:58
- Preserves from evil. . .Exod. 15:26
- Leads to assured hope. . .Heb. 6:11

God rewards. . .Deut. 11:14; Heb. 11:6

49. Discipline of the Church

Ministers authorized to establish. . .Matt. 16:18–19; 18:18
Consists in
- Maintaining sound doctrine. . .1 Tim. 1:3;
  Titus 1:13
- Ordering its affairs. . .1 Cor. 11:34; Titus 1:5
- Rebuking offenders. . .1 Tim. 5:20; 2 Tim. 4:2
- Removing obstinate offenders. . .1 Cor. 5:3–5, 13;
  1 Tim. 1:19–20

Should be submitted to. . .Heb. 13:17

Is for edification. . .2 Cor. 10:8; 13:10

Decency and order, the objects of. . .1 Cor. 14:40

Exercise, in a spirit of charity. . .2 Cor. 2:6–8

50. Disobedience to God

Provokes His anger. . .Ps. 78:10, 40; Isa. 3:8

Forfeits His favor. . .1 Sam. 13:14

Forfeits His promised blessings. . .Josh. 5:6; 1 Sam. 2:30;
   Jer. 18:10

Brings a curse. . .Deut. 11:28; 28:15

Men prone to excuse. . .Gen. 3:11–13

Shall be punished. . .Isa. 42:24–25; Heb. 2:2

Acknowledge the punishment of, to be just. . .
   Neh. 9:32–34; Dan. 9:10–11, 14

Warnings against. . .1 Sam. 12:15; Jer. 12:17

Bitter results of, illustrated. . .Jer. 9:13, 15

Exemplified
  • Adam and Eve. . .Gen. 3:6, 11
  • Moses. . .Num. 20:8, 11, 24
  • Saul. . .1 Sam. 28:18, 20
  • Israel . . .2 Kings 18:9–12
  • Jonah. . .Jon. 1:2–3

51. Divorce

Law of marriage against. . .Gen. 2:24; Matt. 19:6

Not allowed to those who falsely accused their wives. . .
Deut. 22:13–19

Women
- Could obtain. . .Prov. 2:17; Mark 10:12
- Could marry after. . .Deut. 24:1–2
- Responsible for vows after. . .Num. 30:9
- Married after, could not return to first husband. . .
Deut. 24:3–4; Jer. 3:1
- Afflicted by. . .Isa. 54:4, 6

Priests not to marry women after. . .Lev. 21:1, 13–14

Of servants, regulated by law. . .Exod. 21:7, 11

Of captives, regulated by law. . .Deut. 21:13–14

Forced on those who had idolatrous wives. . .Ezra 10:2–19;
Neh. 13:23, 30

Jews condemned for love of. . .Mal. 2:14–16

Forbidden by Christ except for adultery. . .
Matt. 5:32; 19:9

Illustrative of God's casting off of the Jewish church. . .
Isa. 50:1; Jer. 3:8

52. Doctrines

Doctrines, False

Destructive to faith. . .2 Tim. 2:18

Hateful to God. . .Rev. 2:14–15

Try, by scripture. . .Isa. 8:20; 1 John 4:1

Punishment on those who teach. . .Mic. 3:6–7;
2 Pet. 2:1, 3

Doctrines of the Gospel, The
Are from God. . .John 7:16; Acts 13:12
Are taught by scripture. . .2 Tim. 3:16
Lead to fellowship with the Father and with the Son. . .
1 John 1:3; 2 John 1:9
Lead to holiness. . .Rom. 6:17–22; Titus 2:12
Saints obey, from the heart. . .Rom. 6:17
Saints abide in. . .Acts 2:42
A faithful walk adorns. . .Titus 2:10

53. *Drunkenness*

Forbidden. . .Eph. 5:18
Caution against. . .Luke 21:34
Leads to
- Poverty. . .Prov. 21:17; 23:21
- Strife. . .Prov. 23:29–30
- Woe and sorrow. . .Prov. 23:29–30
- Error. . .Isa. 28:7
- Contempt of God's works. . .Isa. 5:12
- Scorning. . .Hosea 7:5
- Rioting and lewdness. . .Rom. 13:13

Avoid those given to. . .Prov. 23:20; 1 Cor. 5:11
Punishment of. . .Deut. 21:20–21; Joel 1:5–6;
Amos 6:6–7; Matt. 24:49–51

54. Edification

Described. . .Eph. 4:12–16

Is the object of

- The ministerial office. . .Eph. 4:11–12
- Ministerial gifts. . .1 Cor. 14:3–5, 12
- Ministerial authority. . .2 Cor. 10:8; 13:10
- The Church's union in Christ. . .Eph. 4:16

The gospel, the instrument of. . .Acts 20:32

Love leads to. . .1 Cor. 8:1

Exhortation to. . .Jude 20–22

Mutual, commanded. . .Rom. 14:19; 1 Thess. 5:11

All to be done to. . .2 Cor. 12:19; Eph. 4:29

Use self-denial to promote, in others. . .1 Cor. 10:23, 33

The peace of the Church favors. . .Acts 9:31

55. Election

Of Christ, as Messiah. . .Isa. 42:1; 1 Pet. 2:6

Of good angels. . .1 Tim. 5:21

Of Israel. . .Deut. 7:6; Isa. 45:4

Of ministers. . .Luke 6:13; Acts 9:10–15

Of churches. . .1 Pet. 5:13

Of saints, is

- Of God. . .1 Thess. 1:4; Titus 1:1
- By Christ. . .John 13:3–4, 18; 15:16
- According to the purpose of God. . .Rom. 9:11;
  Eph. 1:11

- Eternal. . .Eph. 1:4
- Irrespective of what is deserved. . .Rom. 9:11
- Of grace. . .Rom. 11:5
- Recorded in heaven. . .Luke 10:20
- For the glory of God. . .Eph. 1:6
- Through faith. . .2 Thess. 2:13

Should lead to cultivation of graces. . .Col. 3:12

Should be evidenced by diligence. . .2 Pet. 1:10

Saints may have assurance of. . .1 Thess. 1:4

56. Enemies

Christ prayed for His. . .Luke 23:34

Should be
- Loved. . .Matt. 5:44
- Prayed for. . .Acts 7:59–60
- Assisted. . .Prov. 25:21; Rom. 12:20
- Overcome by kindness. . .1 Sam. 26:21

Do not rejoice at the misfortunes of. . .Job 31:29–30

Do not rejoice at the failings of. . .Prov. 24:17

Do not desire the death of. . .1 Kings 3:11

Do not curse. . .Job 31:30

Be concerned for. . .Ps. 35:11–13

God defends against. . .Ps. 59:1, 9; 61:3

God delivers from. . .1 Sam. 12:11; Ezra 8:31; Ps. 18:48

Made to be at peace with saints. . .Prov. 16:7

Pray for deliverance from. . .1 Sam. 12:10;
    Ps. 17:9, 13; 59:1; 64:1

Of saints, God will destroy. . .Ps. 60:12

Praise God for deliverance from. . .Ps. 136:1, 24

57. Entertainments

Given on occasions of
- Marriage. . .Matt. 22:2–3
- Birthdays. . .Mark 6:21
- Parting with friends. . .1 Kings 19:19–21
- Return of friends. . .2 Sam. 12:4; Luke 15:23–24
- Coronation of kings. . .1 Kings 1:9, 18–19;
  1 Chron. 12:38–40; Hosea 7:5
- National deliverance. . .Esther 8:17; 9:17–19

Forwardness to take chief seats at, condemned. . .
    Matt. 23:2, 6; Luke 14:7–8

Offense given by refusing to go to. . .Luke 14:18, 24

None admitted to, after the master had risen and shut
    the door. . .Luke 13:24–25

Began with thanksgiving. . .1 Sam. 9:13; Mark 8:6

Concluded with a hymn. . .Mark 14:22–26

None asked to eat or drink more than he liked at. . .
    Esther 1:8

Music and dancing often introduced at. . .Amos 6:4–5;
    Mark 6:21–22; Luke 15:25

58. Envy

Forbidden. . .Prov. 3:31; Rom. 13:13

Produced by foolish disputation. . .1 Tim. 6:4

Evoked by good deeds of others. . .Eccles. 4:4

A work of the flesh. . .Gal. 5:19, 21; James 4:5

Hurtful to the envious. . .Job 5:2; Prov. 14:30

None can stand before. . .Prov. 27:4

A proof of carnal-mindedness. . .1 Cor. 3:1, 3

Inconsistent with the gospel. . .James 3:14–15

Hinders growth in grace. . .1 Pet. 2:1–2

The wicked

- Are full of. . .Rom. 1:18, 29
- Live in. . .Titus 3:3

Leads to every evil work. . .James 3:16

Punishment of. . .Isa. 26:11

59. Example of Christ, The

Is perfect. . .Heb. 7:26

Conformity to, required in

- Holiness. . .1 Pet. 1:15–16; Rom. 1:4–6
- Righteousness. . .1 John 2:6
- Purity. . .1 John 3:3
- Love. . .John 13:34; Eph. 5:2; 1 John 3:16
- Humility. . .Luke 22:27; Phil. 2:5, 7
- Meekness. . .Matt. 11:29
- Obedience. . .John 15:10

- Self-denial. . .Matt. 16:24; Rom. 15:3
- Benevolence. . .Acts 20:35; 2 Cor. 8:7, 9
- Forgiving others. . .Col. 3:13
- Being not of the world. . .John 17:16
- Suffering wrongfully. . .1 Pet. 2:21–23
- Suffering for righteousness. . .Heb. 12:3–4

60. Faith

◇◇◇◇◇◇◇◇◇◇◇◇◇◇◇◇◇◇◇◇◇◇◇◇◇◇◇◇◇◇◇◇◇◇◇◇◇◇◇

Is the substance of things hoped for. . .Heb. 11:1

Is the evidence of things not seen. . .Heb. 11:1

Commanded. . .Mark 11:22; 1 John 3:23

Christ is the Author and Finisher of. . .Heb. 12:2

Is a gift of the Holy Spirit. . .1 Cor. 12:9

The scriptures designed to produce. . .John 20:31;
    2 Tim. 3:15

Preaching designed to produce. . .John 17:20;
    Acts 8:12; Rom. 10:14–15, 17; 1 Cor. 3:5

Impossible to please God without. . .Heb. 11:6

Justification is by, to be of grace. . .Rom. 4:16

Essential to the profitable reception of the gospel. . .
    Heb. 4:2

Necessary in the Christian warfare. . .
    1 Tim. 1:18–19; 6:12

The gospel effectual in those who have. . .1 Thess. 2:13

Necessary in prayer. . .Matt. 21:22; James 1:6

An evidence of the new birth. . .1 John 5:1

61. Faithfulness

A characteristic of saints. . .Eph. 1:1; Col. 1:2;
1 Tim. 6:2; Rev. 17:14

Exhibited in

- Declaring the Word of God. . .Jer. 23:28;
  2 Cor. 2:17; 4:2
- Helping the brethren. . .3 John 5
- Situations of trust. . .2 Kings 12:15; Neh. 13:13;
  Acts 6:1–3
- Doing work. . .2 Chron. 34:12
- Keeping secrets. . .Prov. 11:13
- The smallest matters. . .Luke 16:10–12

Should be to death. . .Rev. 2:10

Blessedness of. . .1 Sam. 26:23; Prov. 28:20

Faithfulness of God, The

Is part of His character. . .Isa. 49:7; 1 Cor. 1:9;
1 Thess. 5:24

Declared to be

- Great. . .Lam. 3:23
- Incomparable. . .Ps. 89:8
- Unfailing. . .Ps. 89:33; 2 Tim. 2:13
- Infinite. . .Ps. 36:5
- Everlasting. . .Ps. 119:90; 146:6

Should be proclaimed. . .Ps. 40:10; 89:1

62. Fall of Man, The

By the disobedience of Adam. . .Gen. 3:6, 11–12;
   Rom. 5:12, 15, 19
Through temptation of the devil. . .Gen. 3:1–6;
   2 Cor. 11:3; 1 Tim. 2:14
Man in consequence of
* Born in sin. . .Job 15:14; 25:4; Ps. 51:5; Isa. 48:8;
   John 3:6
* Comes short of God's glory. . .Rom. 3:23
* Unrighteous. . .Eccles. 7:20; Rom. 3:10
* Corrupt in speech. . .Rom. 3:13–14
* Devoid of the fear of God. . .Rom. 3:18
Dead in sin. . .Eph. 2:1; Col. 2:13
All men partake of the effects of. . .1 Kings 8:46;
   Gal. 3:22; 1 John 1:8; 5:19
Cannot be remedied by man. . .Prov. 20:9;
   Jer. 2:22; 13:23
Remedy for, provided by God. . .Gen. 3:15; John 3:16

63. Families

Of saints blessed. . .Ps. 128:3–6
Should
* Be taught the scriptures. . .Deut. 4:9–10
* Worship God together. . .1 Cor. 16:19
* Be duly regulated. . .Prov. 31:27;
   1 Tim. 3:4–5, 12

- Live in unity. . .Gen. 45:24; Ps. 133:1
- Rejoice together before God. . .Deut. 14:26

Warning against departing from God. . .Deut. 29:18

Good, exemplified
- Abraham. . .Gen. 18:19
- Job. . .Job 1:5
- Lazarus of Bethany. . .John 11:1–5
- Jailor of Philippi. . .Acts 16:27, 31–34

64. *Fasting*

Spirit of, explained. . .Isa . 58:6–7

Not to be made a subject of display. . .Matt. 6:16–18

Should be to God. . .Zech. 7:5; Matt. 6:18

For the chastening of the soul. . .Ps. 69:10

For the humbling of the soul. . .Ps. 35:13

Observed on occasions of
- Judgments of God. . .Joel 1:14–15; 2:12–13
- Public calamities. . .2 Sam. 1:12
- Afflictions of the church. . .Luke 5:33–35
- Afflictions of others. . .Ps. 35:13; Dan. 6:17–18
- Private afflictions. . .2 Sam. 12:16

Accompanied by
- Prayer. . .Ezra 8:23; Dan. 9:3
- Confession of sin. . .1 Sam. 7:6; Neh. 9:1–2
- Mourning. . .Joel 2:12
- Humiliation. . .Deut. 9:18; Neh. 9:1

Promises connected with. . .Isa. 58:6–12; Matt. 6:18

65. Fatherless

Find mercy in God. . .Hosea 14:3

God will
- Be a father of. . .Ps. 68:5
- Be a helper of. . .Ps. 10:14
- Hear the cry of. . .Exod. 22:22–23
- Execute the judgment of. . .Deut. 10:18; Ps. 10:18
- Punish those who oppress. . .Exod. 22:22–24;
  Isa. 10:1–3; Mal. 3:5

Visit in affliction. . .James 1:27

Let them share in our blessings. . .Deut. 14:29

Defend. . .Ps. 82:3; Isa. 1:17

Don't defraud. . .Prov. 23:10

Don't afflict. . .Exod. 22:22

Don't oppress. . .Zech. 7:10

Do no violence to. . .Jer. 22:3

Blessedness of taking care of. . .Deut. 14:29;
  Job 29:12–13; Jer. 7:6–7

Promises with respect to. . .Jer. 49:11

66. Favor of God, The

Christ the special object of. . .Luke 2:52

Is the source of
- Mercy. . .Isa. 60:10
- Spiritual life. . .Ps. 30:5

Spiritual wisdom leads to. . .Prov. 8:35

Mercy and truth lead to. . .Prov. 3:3–4

Domestic blessings traced to. . .Prov. 18:22

Disappointment of enemies an assured evidence of. . .
Ps. 41:11

Given in answer to prayer. . .Job 33:26

Pray for. . .Ps. 106:4; 119:58

Plead, in prayer. . .Exod. 33:12; Num. 11:15

To be acknowledged. . .Ps. 85:1

67. Fear

Fear, Godly

Searching the scriptures gives the understanding of. . .
Prov. 2:3–5

Described as

- Hatred of evil. . .Prov. 8:13
- Wisdom. . .Job 28:28; Ps. 111:10
- A treasure to saints. . .Prov. 15:16; Isa. 33:6
- A fountain of life. . .Prov. 14:27

Commanded. . .Deut. 13:4; Ps. 22:23; Eccles. 12:13;
1 Pet. 2:17

A characteristic of saints. . .Mal. 3:16

Should accompany the joy of saints. . .Ps. 2:11

Fear, Unholy

A characteristic of the wicked. . .Rev. 21:8

A guilty conscience leads to. . .Gen. 3:8, 10; Ps. 53:5;
Prov. 28:1

Saints sometimes tempted to. . .Ps. 55:5

Saints delivered from. . .Prov. 1:33; Isa. 14:3

Trust in God, a preservative from. . .Ps. 27:1

Exhortations against. . .Isa. 8:12; John 14:27

68. Flattery

<<<<<<<<<<<<<<<<<<<<<<<<<<<<<<<<<<<<<<<

Saints should not use. . .Job 32:21–22

Ministers should not use. . .1 Thess. 2:4–5

The wicked use, to

- Others. . .Ps. 5:9; 12:2
- Themselves. . .Ps. 36:2

Hypocrites use, to

- God. . .Ps. 78:36
- Those in authority. . .Dan. 11:33–34

False prophets and teachers use. . .Ezek. 12:24;
  Rom. 16:18

Wisdom, a preservative against. . .Prov. 4:5

Worldly advantage obtained by. . .Dan. 11:21–22

Seldom gains respect. . .Prov. 28:23

Avoid those given to. . .Prov. 20:19

Danger of. . .Prov. 7:21–23; 29:5

Punishment of. . .Job 17:5; Ps. 12:3

69. Fools

All men are, without the knowledge of God...Titus 3:3

Deny God...Ps. 14:1; 53:1

Blaspheme God...Ps. 74:18

Reproach God...Ps. 74:22

Mock sin...Prov. 14:9

Despise instruction...Prov. 1:7; 15:5

Hate knowledge...Prov. 1:22

Don't delight in understanding...Prov. 18:2

Engage in mischief...Prov. 10:23

Walk in darkness...Eccles. 2:14

Come to shame...Prov. 3:35

Destroy themselves by their speech...Prov. 10:8, 14; Eccles. 10:12

Depend upon their wealth...Luke 12:20

Avoid them...Prov. 9:6; 14:7

Punishment of...Ps. 107:17; Prov. 19:29; 26:10

70. Forgetting God

A characteristic of the wicked...Prov. 2:12, 17; Isa. 65:11

Backsliders are guilty of...Jer. 3:21–22

Is forgetting His

- Covenant...Deut. 4:23; 2 Kings 17:38
- Works...Ps. 78:7, 11; 106:13
- Benefits...Ps. 103:2; 106:7
- Word...Heb. 12:5; James 1:25

- Law. . .Ps. 119:153, 176; Hosea 4:6
- Past deliverance. . .Judg. 8:34; Ps. 78:42
- Power to deliver. . .Isa. 51:13–15

Prosperity often leads to. . .Deut. 8:12–14; Hosea 13:6

Trials should not lead to. . .Ps. 44:17–20

Resolve against. . .Ps. 119:16, 93

Cautions against. . .Deut. 6:12; 8:11

Exhortation to those guilty of. . .Ps. 50:22

Punishment of. . .Job 8:12–13; Ps. 9:17; Isa. 17:10–11; Ezek. 23:35; Hosea 8:14

71. Forgiveness of Wrongs

Christ set an example of. . .Luke 23:34

Commanded. . .Mark 11:25; Rom. 12:19

To be unlimited. . .Matt. 18:21–22; Luke 17:4

Motives to
- The mercy of God. . .Luke 6:36
- Our need of forgiveness. . .Mark 11:25
- God's forgiveness of us. . .Eph. 4:32
- Christ's forgiveness of us. . .Col. 3:13

Should be accompanied by
- Forbearance. . .Col. 3:13
- Kindness. . .Gen. 45:4–11; Rom. 12:20
- Blessing and prayer. . .Matt. 5:44

Promises to. . .Matt. 6:14; Luke 6:37

No forgiveness without. . .Matt. 6:15; James 2:13

72. Forsaking God

Idolaters guilty of. . .1 Sam. 8:8; 1 Kings 11:33

The wicked guilty of. . .Deut. 28:20

Backsliders guilty of. . .Jer. 15:6

Trusting in man is. . .Jer. 17:5

Leads men to follow their own devices. . .Jer. 2:13

Prosperity tempts to. . .Deut. 31:20; 32:15

Brings confusion. . .Jer. 17:13

Brings down His wrath. . .Ezra 8:22

Provokes God to forsake men. . .Judg. 10:13;
    2 Chron. 15:2; 24:20, 24

Resolve against. . .Josh. 24:16; Neh. 10:29–39

Curse pronounced upon. . .Jer. 17:5

Sin of, to be confessed. . .Ezra 9:10

Warnings against. . .Josh. 24:20; 1 Chron. 28:9

Punishment of. . .Deut. 28:20; 2 Kings 22:16–17;
    Isa. 1:28; Jer. 1:16; 5:19

73. Gentiles

Comprehend all nations except the Jews. . .
    Rom. 2:9; 3:9; 9:24

Called

• Heathen. . .Ps. 2:1; Gal. 3:8

• Strangers. . .Isa. 14:1; 60:10

Ruled by God. . .2 Chron. 20:6; Ps. 47:8

Chastised by God. . .Ps. 9:5; 94:10

Hated and despised the Jews. . .Esther 9:1, 5;
   Ps. 44:13–14; 123:3

Often ravaged and defiled the holy land and sanctuary. . .
   Ps. 79:1; Lam. 1:10

Excluded from Israel's privileges. . .Eph. 2:11–12

Given to Christ as His inheritance. . .Ps. 2:8

Christ given as a light to. . .
   Isa. 42:6; Luke 2:21, 25, 27–28, 32

Conversion of, predicted. . .Isa. 2:2; 11:10–11

The gospel not to be preached to, till preached to the
   Jews. . .Matt. 10:5–6; Luke 24:47; Acts 13:46

74. Gift of the Holy Spirit, The

By the Father. . .Neh. 9:20; Luke 11:13

By the Son. . .John 20:21–22

To Christ without measure. . .John 3:34

Given

- According to promise. . .Acts 2:38–39
- Through the intercession of Christ. . .John 14:16
- In answer to prayer. . .Luke 11:13; Eph. 1:16–17
- For instruction. . .Neh. 9:20
- To those who repent and believe. . .Acts 2:38
- To those who obey God. . .Acts 5:32

Is abundant. . .Ps. 68:9; John 7:38–39

Is permanent. . .Isa. 59:21; Hag. 2:5; 1 Pet. 4:14

Is fruit-bearing. . .Isa. 32:15

Received through faith. . .Gal. 3:14

75. Gifts of God, The

All blessings are. . .James 1:17; 2 Pet. 1:3

Are dispensed according to His will. . .Eccles. 2:26; Dan. 2:21; Rom. 12:6; 1 Cor. 7:7

Are free and abundant. . .Num. 14:8; Rom. 8:32

Spiritual

- Are through Christ. . .Ps. 68:18; Eph. 4:7–8; John 6:27
- The Holy Spirit. . .Luke 11:13; Acts 8:19–20
- Grace. . .Ps. 84:11; James 4:6
- Wisdom. . .Prov. 2:6; James 1:5
- Faith. . .Eph. 2:8; Phil. 1:29
- Peace. . .Ps. 29:11
- Eternal life. . .Rom. 6:23

Temporal

- Life. . .Isa. 42:5
- Food and clothing. . .Matt. 6:25–33

Wisdom. . .2 Chron. 1:12

All good things. . .Ps. 34:10; 1 Tim. 6:17

To be used and enjoyed. . .Eccles. 3:13; 5:19–20; 1 Tim. 4:4–5

Should cause us to remember God. . .Deut. 8:18

76. Glorifying God

Commanded. . .1 Chron. 16:28; Ps. 22:23; Isa. 42:12

Due to Him. . .1 Chron. 16:29

For His
- Holiness. . .Ps. 99:9; Rev. 15:4
- Mercy and truth. . .Ps. 115:1; Rom. 15:9
- Wondrous works. . .Matt. 15:31; Acts 4:21
- Deliverance. . .Ps. 50:15
- Grace to others. . .Acts 11:18; 2 Cor. 9:13;
  Gal. 1:24

Christ, an example of. . .John 17:4

Accomplished by
- Relying on His promises. . .Rom. 4:20
- Praising Him. . .Ps. 50:23
- Confessing Christ. . .Phil. 2:11
- Patience in affliction. . .Isa. 24:15
- Faithfulness. . .1 Pet. 4:11

All the blessings of God are designed to lead to. . .
  Isa. 60:21; 61:3

The holy example of saints may lead others to. . .
  Matt. 5:16; 1 Pet. 2:12

77. Glory

◇◇◇◇◇◇◇◇◇◇◇◇◇◇◇◇◇◇◇◇◇◇◇◇◇◇◇◇◇◇◇◇◇◇

God is, to His people. . .Ps. 3:3; Zech. 2:5

Christ is, to His people. . .Isa. 60:1; Luke 2:32

The joy of saints is full of. . .1 Pet. 1:8

The bodies of saints shall be raised in. . .1 Cor. 15:42–43;
Phil. 3:21

Seek not, from man. . .Matt. 6:2; 1 Thess. 2:6

Glory of God, The

Exhibited in Christ. . .John 1:14; 2 Cor. 4:6; Heb. 1:3

Saints desire to behold. . .Ps. 63:2; 90:16

Reverence. . .Isa. 59:19

Plead in prayer. . .Ps. 79:9

Declare. . .1 Chron. 16:24; Ps. 145:5, 11

Magnify. . .Ps. 57:5

The earth is full of. . .Isa. 6:3

78. Gluttony

◇◇◇◇◇◇◇◇◇◇◇◇◇◇◇◇◇◇◇◇◇◇◇◇◇◇◇◇◇◇◇◇◇◇

Christ was falsely accused of. . .Matt. 11:19

The wicked addicted to. . .Phil. 3:19; Jude 12

Leads to poverty. . .Prov. 23:21

Is inconsistent in saints. . .1 Pet. 4:3

Caution against. . .Prov. 23:2–3; Luke 21:34;
Rom. 13:13–14

Pray against temptations to. . .Ps. 141:4

Punishment of. . .Num. 11:33–34; Ps. 78:31;
Deut. 20–21; Amos 6:4, 7

Danger of, illustrated. . .Luke 12:45–46

Exemplified

- Esau. . .Gen. 25:30–34; Heb. 12:16–17
- Israel. . .Num. 11:4; Ps. 78:18
- Sons of Eli. . .1 Sam. 2:12–17

79. God

◇◇◇◇◇◇◇◇◇◇◇◇◇◇◇◇◇◇◇◇◇◇◇◇◇◇◇◇◇◇◇◇◇◇◇◇◇

Goodness of God, The

Is part of His character. . .Ps. 25:8; Nah. 1:7;
Matt. 19:17

Declared to be

- Great. . .Neh. 9:35; Zech. 9:17
- Abundant. . .Exod. 34:6; Ps. 33:5
- Satisfying. . .Ps. 65:4; Jer. 31:12, 14
- Enduring. . .Ps. 23:6; 52:1

Manifested

- To His Church. . .Ps. 31:19; Lam. 3:25
- In providing for the poor. . .Ps. 68:10
- In forgiving sins. . .2 Chron. 30:18; Ps. 86:5

Leads to repentance. . .Rom. 2:4

Reverence. . .Jer. 33:9; Hosea 3:5

Magnify. . .Ps. 107:8; Jer. 33:11

80. Gospel, The

Is good tidings of great joy for all people. . .
    Luke 2:10–11, 31–32
Foretold. . .Isa. 41:27; 52:7; 61:1–3; Mark 1:15
Exhibits the grace of God. . .Acts 14:3; 20:32
Is the power of God to salvation. . .Rom. 1:16;
    1 Cor. 1:18; 1 Thess. 1:5
Is everlasting. . .1 Pet. 1:25; Rev. 14:6
Must be believed. . .Mark 1:15; Heb. 4:2
Brings peace. . .Luke 2:10, 14; Eph. 6:15
Produces hope. . .Col. 1:23
There is fullness of blessing in. . .Rom. 15:29
Promises to sufferers. . .Mark 8:35; 10:30
Awful consequences of not obeying. . .2 Thess. 1:8–9

81. Grace

God is the God of all. . .1 Pet. 5:10
God is the giver of. . .Ps. 84:11; James 1:17
God's throne, the throne of. . .Heb. 4:16
The Holy Spirit is the Spirit of. . .Zech. 12:10;
    Heb. 10:29
Christ was full of. . .John 1:14
Came by Christ. . .John 1:17; Rom. 5:15
Riches of, exhibited in God's kindness through Christ. . .
    Eph. 2:7
Glory of, exhibited in our acceptance in Christ. . .
    Eph. 1:6

The gospel, a declaration of. . .Acts 20:24, 32
God's work completed in saints by. . .2 Thess. 1:11–12
Inheritance of the promises by. . .Rom. 4:16

82. Happiness

Happiness, of Saints in This Life
Is in God. . .Ps. 73:25–26
Only found in the ways of wisdom. . .Prov. 3:13, 17–18
Described by Christ in the beatitudes. . .Matt. 5:3–12
Is derived from
- Trust in God. . .Prov. 16:20; Phil. 4:6–7
- Obedience to God. . .Ps. 40:8; John 13:17
- Finding wisdom. . .Prov. 3:13
Is abundant and satisfying. . .Ps. 36:8; 63:5

Happiness of the Wicked, The
Is limited to this life. . .Ps. 17:14; Luke 16:25
Is short. . .Job 20:5
Is uncertain. . .Luke 12:20; James 4:13–14
Is vain. . .Eccles. 2:1; 7:6
Marred by jealousy. . .Esther 5:13
Leads to sorrow. . .Prov. 14:13
Illustrated. . .Ps. 37:35–36; Luke 12:16–20; 16:19–25

83. Hatred

Forbidden. . .Lev. 19:17; Col. 3:8

Is murder. . .1 John 3:15

Stirs up strife. . .Prov. 10:12

Liars prone to. . .Prov. 26:28

Punishment of. . .Ps. 34:21; 44:7; 89:23; Amos 1:11

Is without cause. . .Ps. 69:4; John 15:25

Punishment of. . .Ps. 2:2, 9; 21:8

Hatred to Christ

No escape for those who persevere in. . .1 Cor. 15:25;
    Heb. 10:29–31

Illustrated. . .Luke 19:12–14, 17

Exemplified

- • Chief priests. . .Matt. 27:1–2; Luke 22:2–5
- • Jews. . .Matt. 27:22–23
- • Scribes. . .Mark 11:18; Luke 11:53–54

84. Heart, The

Issues of life are out of. . .Prov. 4:23

No man can cleanse. . .Prov. 20:9

Faith, the means of purifying. . .Acts 15:9

Renewal of, promised under the gospel. . .
    Ezek. 11:19; 36:26

When broken and contrite, not despised by God. . .
    Ps. 51:17

Regard not sin in. . .Ps. 66:18

Heart, Character of the Renewed
Fixed on God. . .Ps. 57:7; 112:7
Honest and good. . .Luke 8:15
Desirous of God. . .Ps. 84:2
Prayerful. . .1 Sam. 1:13; Ps. 27:8

Heart, Character of the Unrenewed
Desperately wicked. . .Jer. 17:9
Far from God. . .Isa. 29:13; Matt. 15:8
Deceived. . .Isa. 44:20; James 1:26
Rebellious. . .Jer. 5:23

85. *Heathen, The*

Are without God and Christ. . .Eph. 2:12
Cautions against imitating. . .Jer. 10:2; Matt. 6:7
God

- Will be exalted among. . .Ps. 46:10; 102:15
- Punishes. . .Ps. 44:2; Joel 3:11–13; Mic. 5:15; Hab. 3:12; Zech. 14:18
- Will finally judge. . .Rom. 2:12–16

Salvation provided for. . .Acts 28:28; Rom. 15:9–12
The glory of God to be declared among. . .
    1 Chron. 16:24; Ps. 96:3
Baptism to be administered to. . .Matt. 28:19
The Holy Spirit poured out upon. . .Acts 10:44–45; 15:8
Pray for. . .Ps. 67:2–5
Aid missions to. . .2 Cor. 11:9; 3 John 1:6–7

Conversion of, acceptable to God. . .Acts 10:35;
   Rom. 15:16

86. Heaven

<<<<<<<<<<<<<<<<<<<<<<<<<<<<<<<<<<<<<<<<<<<

Created by God. . .Gen. 1:1; Rev. 10:6

Everlasting. . .Ps. 89:29; 2 Cor. 5:1

Immeasurable. . .Jer. 31:37

Holy. . .Deut. 26:15; Ps. 20:6; Isa. 57:15

God's dwelling place. . .1 Kings 8:30; Matt. 6:9

God's throne. . .Isa. 66:1; Acts 7:49

Angels are in. . .Matt. 18:10; 24:36

Names of saints are written in. . .Luke 10:20; Heb. 12:23

Saints rewarded in. . .Matt. 5:12; 1 Pet. 1:4

Repentance occasions joy in. . .Luke 15:7

Lay up treasure in. . .Matt. 6:20; Luke 12:33

The wicked excluded from. . .Gal. 5:21; Eph. 5:5;
   Rev. 22:14–15

87. Heedfulness

Commanded. . .Exod. 23:13; Prov. 4:25–27

Necessary
- In the care of the soul. . .Deut. 4:9
- In the house and worship of God. . .Eccles. 5:1
- In what we hear. . .Mark 4:24
- In keeping God's commandments. . .Josh. 22:5
- In conduct. . .Eph. 5:15
- In speech. . .Prov. 13:3; James 1:19
- In worldly company. . .Ps. 39:1; Col. 4:5
- Against sin. . .Heb. 12:15–16
- Against unbelief. . .Heb. 3:12
- Against false Christs, and false prophets. . .
     Matt. 24:4–5, 23–24

Promises to. . .1 Kings 2:4; 1 Chron. 22:13

88. Hell

The place of future punishment
- Destruction from the presence of God. . .
   2 Thess. 1:9
- Prepared for the devil. . .Matt. 25:41
- Devils are confined in, until the Judgment Day. . .
   2 Pet. 2:4; Jude 6

Punishment of, is eternal. . .Isa. 33:14; Rev. 20:10

The wicked shall be condemned to. . .Ps. 9:17

Human power cannot preserve from. . .Ezek. 32:27

The body suffers in. . .Matt. 5:29; 10:28

The soul suffers in. . .Matt. 10:28

The wise avoid. . .Prov. 15:24

Endeavor to keep others from. . .Prov. 23:14; Jude 23

The beast, false prophets, and the devil shall be cast into. . .Rev. 19:20; 20:10

The powers of, cannot prevail against the church. . . Matt. 16:18

Illustrated. . .Isa. 30:33

89. Holiness

Commanded. . .Lev. 11:45; 20:7; Eph. 5:8; Col. 3:12; Rom. 12:1

The character of God, the standard of. . .Lev. 19:2; 1 Pet. 1:15–16; Eph. 5:1

The gospel the way of. . .Isa. 35:8

Necessary to God's worship. . .Ps. 24:3–4

None shall see God without. . .Eph. 5:5; Heb. 12:14

Required in prayer. . .1 Tim. 2:8

Holiness of God, The

Is incomparable. . .Exod. 15:11; 1 Sam. 2:2

Saints are commanded to imitate. . .Lev. 11:44; 1 Pet. 1:15–16

Saints should praise. . .Ps. 30:4

Requires holy service. . .Josh. 24:19; Ps. 93:5

Heavenly hosts adore. . .Isa. 6:3; Rev. 4:8

Should be magnified. . .1 Chron. 16:10; Ps. 48:1; 99:3, 5; Rev. 15:4

90. Holy Spirit, The

Proceeds from the Father. . John 15:26

Sent by Christ from the Father. . John 15:26; 16:7

As equal to, and one with the Father. . .Matt. 28:19;
2 Cor. 13:14

As the source of wisdom. . .1 Cor. 12:8; Isa. 11:2;
John 16:13; 14:26

As dwelling in saints. . John 14:17;
1 Cor. 14:25; 3:16; 6:19

As Comforter of the church. . .Acts 9:31; 2 Cor. 1:3

As convincing of sin, of righteousness, and of
judgment. . John 16:8–11

He creates and gives life. . Job 33:4

He spoke in, and by, the prophets. . .Acts 1:16;
1 Pet. 1:11–12; 2 Pet. 1:21

He glorifies Christ. . John 16:13–14

He has a power of His own. . .Rom. 15:13

As the Spirit of wisdom. . .Isa. 11:2; 40:13–14

91. Holy of Holies

Divided from the outward tabernacle by a veil. . .
Exod. 26:31–33

Contained

- Ark of testimony. . .Exod. 26:33; 40:3, 21
- Mercy seat. . .Exod. 26:34
- Cherubim. . .Exod. 25:18–22; 1 Kings 6:23–28

- Golden censer. . .Heb. 9:3–4
- Pot of manna. . .Exod. 16:33; Heb. 9:4
- Aaron's rod. . .Num. 17:10; Heb. 9:4
- A written copy of the divine law. . .Deut. 31:26; 2 Kings 22:3, 8

God appeared in. . .Exod. 25:22; Lev. 16:2

The priests allowed to enter, and prepare the holy things for removal. . .Num. 4:5

Laid open to view at Christ's death. . .Matt. 27:51

A type of heaven. . .Ps. 102:19; Heb. 9:12–13, 24

Saints have boldness to enter the true. . .Heb. 10:19

92. Hope

In God. . .Ps. 39:7; 1 Pet. 1:21

In Christ. . .1 Cor. 15:19; 1 Tim. 1:1

In God's promises. . .Acts 26:6–7; Titus 1:2

In the mercy of God. . .Ps. 33:18

Is the work of the Holy Spirit. . .Rom. 15:13; Gal. 5:5

Obtained through
- Grace. . .2 Thess. 2:16
- The Word. . .Ps. 119:81
- Patience and comfort of the scriptures. . . Rom. 15:4
- The gospel. . .Col. 1:5, 23
- Faith. . .Rom. 5:1–2; Gal. 5:5

Triumphs over difficulties. . .Rom. 4:18

Leads to patience. . .Rom. 8:25; 1 Thess. 1:3

Be ready to give an answer concerning. . .1 Pet. 3:15

93. Hospitality

Commanded. . .Rom. 12:13; 1 Pet. 4:9

Required in ministers. . .1 Tim. 3:2; Titus 1:7–8

A test of Christian character. . .1 Tim. 5:10

Especially to be shown to

- Strangers. . .Heb. 13:2
- The poor. . .Isa. 58:7; Luke 14:13
- Enemies. . .2 Kings 6:22–23; Rom. 12:20

Encouragement to. . .Luke 14:13–14; Heb. 13:2

Exemplified

- Abraham. . .Gen. 18:3–8
- Lot. . .Gen. 19:2–3
- Laban. . .Gen. 24:31–32
- Shunnamite. . .2 Kings 4:8
- Lydia. . .Acts 16:14–15

94. Humility

Necessary to the service of God. . .Mic. 6:8

Christ an example of. . .Matt. 11:29; John 13:14–15;
Phil. 2:5–8

A characteristic of saints. . .Ps. 34:2

Is before honor. . .Prov. 15:33

Leads to riches, honor, and life. . .Prov. 22:4

Afflictions intended to produce. . .Lev. 26:41;
Deut. 8:3; Lam. 3:20

Humility of Christ, The

Exhibited in His

- Taking our nature. . .Phil. 2:7; Heb. 2:16
- Birth. . .Luke 2:4–7
- Becoming a servant. . .Matt. 20:28; Luke 22:27; Phil. 2:7
- Obedience. . .John 6:38; Heb. 10:9
- Death. . .John 10:15, 17–18; Phil. 2:8; Heb. 12:2

Saints should imitate. . .Phil. 2:5–8

His exaltation, the result of. . .Phil. 2:8–9

95. Husbands

Should have but one wife. . .Gen. 2:24; Mark 10:6–8; 1 Cor. 7:2–4

Have authority over their wives. . .Gen. 3:16; 1 Cor. 11:3; Eph. 5:23

Duty of, to wives

- To respect them. . .1 Pet. 3:7
- To love them. . .Eph. 5:25–33; Col. 3:19
- To regard them as themselves. . .Gen. 2:23; Matt. 19:5
- To be faithful to them. . .Prov. 5:19; Mal. 2:14–15
- To dwell with them for life. . .Gen. 2:24; Matt. 19:3–9
- To comfort them. . .1 Sam. 1:8
- Not to leave them, though unbelieving. . . 1 Cor. 7:11–12, 14, 16

Duties of, not to interfere with their duties to Christ. . .
Luke 14:26; Matt. 19:29

96. Hypocrites

God knows and detects. . .Isa. 29:15–16

God has no pleasure in. . .Isa. 9:17

Shall not come before God. . .Job 13:16

Described as

- Willfully blind. . .Matt. 23:17, 19, 26
- Self-righteous. . .Isa. 65:5; Luke 18:11
- Exact in minor, but neglecting important duties. . .Matt. 23:23–24
- Professing but not practicing. . .Ezek. 33:31–32; Matt. 23:3; Rom. 2:17–23

Destroy others by slander. . .Prov. 11:9

In power, are a snare. . .Job 34:30

Beware the principles of. . .Luke 12:1

Spirit of, hinders growth in grace. . .1 Pet. 2:1

Punishment of. . .Job 15:34; Isa. 10:6; Jer. 42:20, 22; Matt. 24:51

97. Idleness and Sloth

Forbidden. . .Rom. 12:11; Heb. 6:12

Produce apathy. . .Prov. 12:27; 26:15

Accompanied by conceit. . .Prov. 26:16

Lead to

- Poverty. . .Prov. 10:4; 20:13
- Need. . .Prov. 20:4; 24:34
- Hunger. . .Prov. 19:15; 20:13
- Disappointment. . .Prov. 13:4; 21:25
- Ruin. . .Prov. 24:30–31; Eccles. 10:18
- Tattling and meddling. . .1 Tim. 5:13

Effects of, afford instruction to others. . .Prov. 24:30–34

Remonstrance against. . .Prov. 6:6, 9

98. Idolatry

Forbidden. . .Exod. 20:2–3; Deut. 5:7

Is changing the glory of God into an image. . .Rom. 1:23;
Acts 17:29

Is changing the truth of God into a lie. . .Rom. 1:25;
Isa. 44:20

Is a work of the flesh. . .Gal. 5:19–20

Incompatible with the service of God. . .Gen. 35:2–3;
Josh. 24:23; 1 Sam. 7:3; 1 Kings 18:21; 2 Cor. 6:15–16

Warnings against. . .Deut. 4:15–19

Exhortations to turn from. . .Ezek. 14:6; 20:7;
Acts 14:13, 15

Saints refuse to receive the worship of. . .

    Acts 10:25–26; 14:11–15

Angels refuse to receive the worship of. . .Rev. 22:8–9

Everything connected with, should be destroyed. . .

    Exod. 34:13; Deut. 7:5; 2 Sam. 5:21; 2 Kings 23:14

A virtual forsaking of God. . Jer. 2:9–13

99. Industry

Commanded. . .Eph. 4:28; 1 Thess. 4:11

Required of man in a state of innocence. . .Gen. 2:15

Required of man after the fall. . .Gen. 3:23

To be suspended on the Sabbath. . .Exod. 20:10

Characteristic of godly women. . .Prov. 31:13–31

Early rising necessary to. . .Prov. 31:15

Necessary to supply

- Our own wants. . .Acts 20:34; 1 Thess. 2:9
- Wants of others. . .Acts 20:35; Eph. 4:28

The slothful devoid of. . .Prov. 24:30–31

Leads to

- Increase of substance. . .Prov. 13:11
- Affection of relatives. . .Prov. 31:28
- General commendation. . .Prov. 31:31

100. Indwelling of the Holy Spirit, The

In His Church, as His temple. . .1 Cor. 3:16
In the body of saints, as His temple. . .1 Cor. 6:19;
    2 Cor. 6:16
Promised to saints. . .Ezek. 36:27
Saints enjoy. . .Isa. 63:11; 2 Tim. 1:14
Is the means of
  • Reviving. . .Rom. 8:11
  • Guiding. . .John 16:13; Gal. 5:18
  • Fruit-bearing. . .Gal. 5:22
A proof of being Christ's. . .Rom. 8:9; 1 John 4:13
A proof of adoption. . .Rom. 8:15; Gal. 4:5
Is abiding. . .1 John 2:27
Opposed by the carnal nature. . .Gal. 5:17

101. Injustice

Forbidden. . .Lev. 19:15, 35; Deut. 16:19
Specially to be avoided toward
  • The poor. . .Exod. 23:6; Prov. 22:16, 22–23
  • The stranger and fatherless. . .Exod. 22:21–22;
    Deut. 24:17; Jer. 22:3
  • Servants. . .Job 31:13–14; Deut. 24:14; Jer. 22:13
Of the least kind, condemned. . .Luke 16:10
God
  • Does not approve of. . .Lam. 3:35–36
  • Hears the cry of those who suffer. . .James 5:4

- Provoked to avenge. . .Ps. 12:5

Brings a curse. . .Deut. 27:17, 19

A bad example leads to. . .Exod. 23:2

Covetousness leads to. . .Jer. 6:13; Ezek. 22:12; Mic. 2:2

102. Inspiration of the Holy Spirit, The

Foretold. . .Joel 2:28; Acts 2:16–18

All scripture given by. . .2 Sam. 23:2; 2 Tim. 3:16;
2 Pet. 1:21

Design of
- To reveal future events. . .Acts 1:16; 28:25;
1 Pet. 1:11
- To reveal the mysteries of God. . .Amos 3:7;
1 Cor. 2:10
- To direct ministers. . .Ezek. 3:24–27;
Acts 11:12; 13:2
- To control ministers. . .Acts 16:6
- To testify against sin. . .2 Kings 17:13; Neh. 9:30;
Mic. 3:8; John 16:8–9

Modes of
- Various. . .Heb. 1:1
- By a voice. . .Isa. 6:8; Acts 8:29; Rev. 1:10
- By visions. . .Num. 12:6; Ezek. 11:24
- By dreams. . .Num. 12:6; Dan. 7:1

Necessary to prophesying. . .Num. 11:25–27;
2 Chron. 20:14–17

Is irresistible. . .Amos 3:8

Despisers of, punished. . .2 Chron. 36:15–16; Zech. 7:12

103. Joy

God gives. . .Eccles. 2:26; Ps. 4:7

Christ appointed to give. . .Isa. 61:3

Is a fruit of the Spirit. . .Gal. 5:22

Promised to saints. . .Ps. 132:16; Isa. 35:10; 55:12; 56:7

Fullness of, in God's presence. . .Ps. 16:11

Increased to the meek. . .Isa. 29:19

Serve God with. . .Ps. 100:2

Joy of God Over His People, The

Greatness of, described. . .Zeph. 3:17

On account of their

- Repentance. . .Luke 15:7, 10
- Faith. . .Heb. 11:5–6
- Meekness. . .Ps. 149:4
- Uprightness. . .1 Chron. 29:17; Prov. 11:20

104. Judgment, The

A day appointed for. . .Acts 17:31; Rom. 2:16

Time of, unknown to us. . .Mark 13:26–27, 32

Called the

- Day of wrath. . .Rom. 2:5; Rev. 6:17
- Revelation of the righteous judgment of God. . . Rom. 2:5
- Day of judgment and destruction of ungodly men. . .2 Pet. 3:7

- Day of destruction. . .Job 21:30
- Judgment of the great day. . .Jude 6

Saints shall sit with Christ in. . .1 Cor. 6:2; Rev. 20:4

Shall take place at the coming of Christ. . .Matt. 25:31, 46; 2 Tim. 4:1

The books shall be opened at. . .Dan. 7:10

Saints shall be rewarded at. . .2 Tim. 4:8; Rev. 11:18

The wicked shall be condemned in. . .
 Matt. 7:22–23; 25:41

Warn the wicked of. . .Acts 24:25; 2 Cor. 5:11

105. Justice

Commanded. . .Deut. 16:20; Isa. 56:1

Christ, an example of. . .Ps. 98:9; Isa. 11:4; Jer. 23:5

Specially required in rulers. . .2 Sam. 23:3; Ezek. 45:9

God
- Requires. . .Mic. 6:8
- Sets the highest value on. . .Prov. 21:3
- Delights in. . .Prov. 11:1

Brings its own reward. . .Jer. 22:15

Promises to. . .Isa. 33:15–16; Jer. 7:5, 7

Justice of God, The

Is a part of His character. . .Deut. 32:4; Isa. 45:21

Acknowledge. . .Ps. 51:4; Rom. 3:4

Magnify. . .Ps. 98:9; 99:3–4

106. Justification before God

Promised in Christ. . .Isa. 45:25; 53:11
Is the act of God. . .Isa. 50:8; Rom. 8:33
Under law
- Requires perfect obedience. . .Lev. 18:5;
  Rom. 2:13; 10:5; James 2:10
- Man cannot attain to. . .Job 9:2–3, 20; 25:4;
  Ps. 130:3; 143:2; Rom. 3:20; 9:31–32
Under the gospel
- Is not of works. . .Acts 13:39; Rom. 8:3;
  Gal. 2:16; 3:11
- Is by faith alone. . .John 5:24; Acts 13:39;
  Rom. 3:30; 5:1; Gal. 2:16
- Is of grace. . .Rom. 3:24; 4:16; 5:17–21
- In the name of Christ. . .1 Cor. 6:11
- Frees from condemnation. . .Isa. 50:8–9; 54:17;
  Rom. 8:33–34
- Entitles to an inheritance. . .Titus 3:7
The wicked shall not attain to. . .Exod. 23:7

107. Lamb, The

The young of the flock. . .Exod. 12:5; Ezek. 45:15
The shepherd's care for. . .Isa. 40:11
Used for
- Food. . .Deut. 32:14; 2 Sam. 12:4

- Clothing. . .Prov. 27:26
- Sacrifice. . .1 Chron. 29:21; 2 Chron. 29:32

Illustrative

- Of purity of Christ. . .1 Pet. 1:19
- Of Christ as a sacrifice. . John 1:29; Rev. 5:6
- Of the Lord's people. . .Isa. 5:17; 11:6
- (Patience of,) of the patience of Christ. . .
  Isa. 53:7; Acts 8:32
- (Among wolves,) of ministers among the ungodly. . .
  Luke 10:3
- (Brought to slaughter,) of the wicked under
  judgments. . .Jer. 51:40

108. Law of God, The

Is absolute and perpetual. . .Matt. 5:18

Requires perfect obedience. . .Deut. 27:26; Gal. 3:10;
  James 2:10

Designed to lead to Christ. . .Gal. 3:24

Blessedness of keeping. . .Ps. 119:1; Matt. 5:19;
  1 John 3:22, 24; Rev. 22:14

The love of, produces peace. . .Ps. 119:165

Is the rule of life to saints. . .1 Cor. 9:21; Gal. 5:13–14

Punishment for disobeying. . .Neh. 9:26–27;
  Isa. 65:11–13; Jer. 9:13–16

Is the law of God. . .Lev. 26:46

Law of Moses, The

Given

- From the Mount Sinai. . .Exod. 19:11, 20; 20:1–26
- Through Moses as mediator. . .Deut. 5:5, 27–28;
  John 1:17; Gal. 3:19
- To the Jews. . .Lev. 26:46; Ps. 78:5
- After the Exodus. . .Deut. 4:45; Ps. 81:4–5
- To no other nation. . .Deut. 4:8; Ps. 147:20

109. Liberality

Pleasing to God. . .2 Cor. 9:7; Heb. 13:16

God never forgets. . .Heb. 6:10

Christ set an example of. . .2 Cor. 8:9

Characteristic of saints. . .Ps. 112:9; Isa. 32:8

Unprofitable, without love. . .1 Cor. 13:3

Should be exercised

- Toward all men. . .Gal. 6:10
- In forwarding missions. . .Phil. 4:14–16
- Willingly. . .Exod. 25:2; 2 Cor. 8:12
- Abundantly. . .2 Cor. 8:7; 9:11–13

Exercise of, provokes others to. . .2 Cor. 9:2

Blessings connected with. . .Ps. 41:1; Prov. 22:9;
  Acts 20:35

Promises to. . .Ps. 112:9; Prov. 11:25; 28:27;
  Eccles. 11:1–2; Isa. 58:10

Exhortations to. . .Luke 3:11; 11:41; Acts 20:35;
  1 Cor. 16:1; 1 Tim. 6:17–18

110. Liberty, Christian

Through the gospel. . .John 8:32
Proclaimed by Christ. . .Isa. 61:1; Luke 4:18
Is freedom from
- The law. . .Rom. 7:6; 8:2
- The curse of the law. . .Gal. 3:13
- The fear of death. . .Heb. 2:15
- Sin. . .Rom. 6:7, 18
- Corruption. . .Rom. 8:21
- Bondage of man. . .1 Cor. 9:19
- Jewish ordinances. . .Gal. 4:3; Col. 2:20

Saints are called to. . .Gal. 5:13

111. Life, Eternal

To know God and Christ is. . .John 17:3
Given
- By God. . .Ps. 133:3; Rom. 6:23
- Through Christ. . .Rom. 5:21; 6:23
- To those who believe in Christ. . .
  John 3:15–16; 6:40, 47

Life, Natural

God is the author of. . .Gen. 2:7; Acts 17:28
God preserves. . .Ps. 36:6; 66:9
Is in the hand of God. . .Job 12:10; Dan. 5:23
Of others, not to be taken away. . .Exod. 20:13

Life, Spiritual

God is the Author of. . .Ps. 36:9; Col. 2:13

Is hidden with Christ. . .Col. 3:3

Saints praise God for. . .Ps. 119:175

Seek to grow in. . .Eph. 4:15; 1 Pet. 2:2

112. *Light*

God the only source of. . .James 1:17

Created by God. . .Gen. 1:3; Isa. 45:7

Separated from darkness. . .Gen. 1:4

Illustrative of

- Glory of God. . .Ps. 104:2; 1 Tim. 6:16
- Wisdom of God. . .Dan. 2:22
- Favor of God. . .Ps. 4:6; Isa. 2:5
- Word of God. . .Ps. 119:105, 130; 2 Pet. 1:19
- Gospel. . .2 Cor. 4:4; 1 Pet. 2:9
- Saints. . .Luke 16:8; Eph. 5:8; Phil. 2:15
- The path of the just. . .Prov. 4:18
- The glory of the church. . .Isa. 60:1–3

113. *Long-Suffering of God, The*

Is part of His character. . .Exod. 34:6; Num. 14:18;
    Ps. 86:15

Salvation, the object of. . .2 Pet. 3:15

Through Christ's intercession. . .Luke 13:6–9

Should lead to repentance. . .Rom. 2:4; 2 Pet. 3:9

An encouragement to repent. . .Joel 2:13

Exhibited in forgiving sins. . .Rom. 3:25

Exercised toward
- His people. . .Isa. 30:18; Ezek. 20:17
- The wicked. . .Rom. 9:22; 1 Pet. 3:20

Plead in prayer. . .Jer. 15:15

Limits set to. . .Gen. 6:3; Jer. 44:22

Illustrated. . .Luke 13:6, 9

114. *Love, of Christ*

To the Father. . .Ps. 91:14; John 14:31

To His church. . .Song of Sol. 4:8–9; 5:1; John 15:9; Eph. 5:25

Love, of God

To those who love Him. . .Prov. 8:17; John 14:21

Passes knowledge. . .Eph. 3:19

Is a part of His character. . .2 Cor. 13:11; 1 John 4:8

Irrespective of merit. . .Deut. 7:7; Job 7:17

Love to Christ

His love to us a motive to. . .2 Cor. 5:14

A characteristic of saints. . .Song of Sol. 1:4

Love to God

The first great commandment. . .Matt. 22:37–38

With all the heart. . .Deut. 6:5; Matt. 22:37

Better than all sacrifices. . .Mark 12:33

Promises connected with. . .Deut. 11:13–15; Ps. 69:36;
Isa. 56:6–7; James 1:12

Love to Man

After the example of Christ. . .John 13:34; 15:12;
Eph. 5:2

Is the second great commandment. . .Matt. 22:37–39

115. Lying

Forbidden. . .Lev. 19:11; Col. 3:9

A hindrance to prayer. . .Isa. 59:2–3

The devil, the father of. . .John 8:44

Leads to

- Hatred. . .Prov. 26:28
- Love of impure conversation. . .Prov. 17:4

Often accompanied by gross crimes. . .Hosea 4:1–2

Folly of concealing hatred by. . .Prov. 10:18

Vanity of getting riches by. . .Prov. 21:6

Shall be detected. . .Prov. 12:19

Poverty preferable to. . .Prov. 19:22

Excludes from heaven. . .Rev. 21:27; 22:14–15

Punishment for. . .Ps. 5:6; 120:3–4; Prov. 19:5; Jer. 50:36

116. Malice

Springs from an evil heart. . .Matt. 15:19–20;
   Gal. 5:19–20

Forbidden. . .1 Cor. 14:20; Col. 3:8; Eph. 4:26–27

A hindrance to growth in grace. . .1 Pet. 2:1–2

Incompatible with the worship of God. . .1 Cor. 5:7–8

Saints avoid. . .Job 31:29–30; Ps. 35:12–14

The wicked

- Speak with. . .3 John 10
- Live in. . .Titus 3:3
- Filled with. . .Rom. 1:29, 32

Pray for those who injure you through. . .Matt. 5:44

Brings its own punishment. . .Ps. 7:15–16

God avenges. . .Ps. 10:14; Ezek. 36:5

Punishment of. . .Amos 1:11–12; Obad. 1:10–15

117. Marriage

Divinely instituted. . .Gen. 2:24

A covenant relationship. . .Mal. 2:4

Designed for

- The happiness of man. . .Gen. 2:18
- Increasing the human population. . .Gen. 1:28; 9:1

Should be only in the Lord. . .1 Cor. 7:39

Indissoluble during the joint lives of the parties. . .
   Matt. 19:6; Rom. 7:2–3; 1 Cor. 7:39

Celebrated

- With great rejoicing. . .Jer. 33:11; John 3:29
- With feasting. . .Gen. 29:21–22; Judg. 14:7–10;
  Matt. 22:2–3; John 2:1–10

Illustrative of
- God's union with the Jewish nation. . .Isa. 54:5;
  Jer. 3:14; Hosea 2:19–20
- Christ's union with His church. . .Eph. 5:23–24, 32

118. Meekness

Christ set an example of. . .Ps. 45:4; Isa. 53:7;
  Matt. 11:29; 21:5; 2 Cor. 10:1; 1 Pet. 2:21–23

Jesus' teaching. . .Matt. 5:38–45

A fruit of the Spirit. . .Gal. 5:22–23

Precious in the sight of God. . .1 Pet. 3:4

A characteristic of wisdom. . .James 3:17

Necessary to a Christian walk. . .Eph. 4:1–2; 1 Cor. 6:7

Those who are gifted with
- Are exalted. . .Ps. 147:6; Matt. 23:12
- Are richly provided for. . .Ps. 22:26
- Increase their joy. . .Isa. 29:19
- Shall inherit the earth. . .Ps. 37:11

Blessedness of. . .Matt. 5:5

119. Mercy

After the example of God. . .Luke 6:36

Commanded. . .2 Kings 6:21–23; Hosea 12:6;
   Rom. 12:20–21; Col. 3:12

To be engraved on the heart. . .Prov. 3:3

Characteristic of saints. . .Ps. 37:26; Isa. 57:1

Should be shown with cheerfulness. . .Rom. 12:8

Mercy of God, The

Is part of His character. . .Exod. 34:6–7; Ps. 62:12;
   Neh. 9:17; Jon. 4:2, 10–11; 2 Cor. 1:3

Is His delight. . .Mic. 7:18

Should be

- Sought for ourselves. . .Ps. 6:2
- Sought for others. . .Gal. 6:16; 1 Tim. 1:2;
  2 Tim. 1:18
- Pleaded in prayer. . .Ps. 6:4; 25:6; 51:1
- Rejoiced in. . .Ps. 31:7

120. Ministers

Called by God. . .Exod. 28:1; Heb. 5:4

Qualified by God. . .Isa. 6:5–7; 2 Cor. 3:5–6

Commissioned by Christ. . .Matt. 28:19

Sent by the Holy Spirit. . .Acts 13:2, 4

Have authority from God. . .2 Cor. 10:8; 13:10

Entrusted with the gospel. . .1 Thess. 2:4

Specially protected by God. . .2 Cor. 1:10

Labors of, vain, without God's blessing. . .1 Cor. 3:7; 15:10

Compared to earthen vessels. . .2 Cor. 4:7

Should be

- Pure. . .Isa. 52:11; 1 Tim. 3:9
- Holy. . .Exod. 28:35–36; Lev. 21:6; Titus 1:7–8
- Humble. . .Acts 20:19

Should seek the salvation of their flock. . .1 Cor. 10:33

121. Miracles

Power of God necessary for. . .John 3:2

Described as

- Marvelous things. . .Ps. 78:12
- Marvelous works. . .Isa. 29:14; Ps. 105:5
- Signs and wonders. . .Jer. 32:21; John 4:48;
  2 Cor. 12:12

Miracles of Christ, The

His resurrection. . .Luke 24:1–6; John 10:18

Miracles Through Evil Agents

Performed through the power of the devil. . .2 Thess. 2:9;
  Rev. 16:14

Not to be regarded. . .Deut. 13:3

Deceive the ungodly. . .2 Thess. 2:10–12;
  Rev. 13:14; 19:20

Examples of

- Moses and Aaron overwhelm Egyptians. . .
  Exod. 14:26–28
- The apostles perform any miracles. . .
  Acts 2:43; 5:12

Dispensed according to His sovereign will. . .1 Cor. 12:11

122. *Missionaries, All Christians Should Be*

After the example of Christ. . .Acts 10:38

From their calling as saints. . .Exod. 19:6; 1 Pet. 2:9

As faithful stewards. . .1 Pet. 4:10–11

In first giving their own selves to the Lord. . .2 Cor. 8:5

In declaring what God has done for them. . .Ps. 66:16;
116:16–19

In preferring Christ above all relations. . .Luke 14:26;
1 Cor. 2:2

In forsaking all for Christ. . .Luke 5:11

In holy conservation. . .Ps. 37:30; Prov. 10:31; 15:7;
Eph. 4:29; Col. 4:6

In encouraging the weak. . .Isa. 35:3–4; Rom. 14:1;
15:1; 1 Thess. 5:14

With a willing heart. . .Exod. 35:29; 1 Chron. 29:9, 14

123. Money

Gold and silver used as. . .Gen. 13:2; Num. 22:18

Brass introduced as, by the Romans. . .Matt. 10:9

Of the Romans, stamped with the image of Caesar. . .
Matt. 22:20–21

Usually taken by weight. . .Gen. 23:16; Jer. 32:10

Was current with the merchants. . .Gen. 23:16

Jews forbidden to take interest for. . .Lev. 25:37

Changing of, a trade. . .Matt. 21:12; John 2:15

Custom of presenting a piece of. . .Job 42:11

Power and usefulness of. . .Eccles. 7:12; 10:19

Love of, the root of all evil. . .1 Tim. 6:10

124. Murder

Forbidden by Mosaic law. . .Exod. 20:13; Deut. 5:17

Why forbidden by God. . .Gen. 9:6

The law made to restrain. . .1 Tim. 1:9

Killing a thief in the day, counted as. . .Exod. 22:3

Often committed by night. . .Neh. 6:10; Job 24:14

Mode of clearing those suspected of. . .Deut. 21:3–9;
Matt. 27:24

To be proved by at least two witnesses. . .Num. 35:30;
Deut. 19:11, 15

Forbidden. . .Gen. 9:6; Exod. 20:13; Deut. 5:17;
Rom. 13:9

Explained by Christ. . .Matt. 5:21–22

Hatred is. . .1 John 3:15

Is a work for the flesh. . .Gal. 5:19–21

Comes from the heart. . .Matt. 15:19

Punishment of. . .Gen. 4:12–15; 9:6; Num. 35:30;
    2 Kings 9:36–37; Jer. 19:4–9

125. Murmuring

◇◇◇◇◇◇◇◇◇◇◇◇◇◇◇◇◇◇◇◇◇◇◇◇◇◇◇◇◇◇◇◇◇◇◇◇

Forbidden. . .1 Cor. 10:10; Phil. 2:14

Against
- God. . .Prov. 19:3
- The sovereignty of God. . .Rom. 9:19–20
- Christ. . .Luke 5:30; 15:2; 19:7; John 6:41–43, 52
- Ministers of God. . .Exod. 17:3; Num. 16:41
- Disciples of Christ. . .Mark 7:1–5; Luke 5:30; 6:2

Provokes God. . .Num. 14:2, 11; Deut. 9:8, 22

Saints cease from. . .Isa. 29:23–24

Characteristic of the wicked. . .Jude 16

Guilt of encouraging others in. . .
    Num. 13:31–33; 14:36–37

Punishment of. . .Num. 11:1; 14:27–29; 16:45–46;
    Ps. 106:25–26

Illustrated. . .Matt. 20:11; Luke 15:29–30

126. Music

Early invention of. . .Gen. 4:21

Divided into

- Vocal. . .2 Sam. 19:35; Acts 16:25
- Instrumental. . .Dan. 6:18

Designed to promote joy. . .Eccles. 2:8, 10

Considered effective in mental disorders. . .
1 Sam. 16:14–17, 23

Appointed to be used in the temple. . .
1 Chron. 16:4–6; 23:5–6; 25:1; 2 Chron. 29:25

Generally put aside in times of affliction. . .Ps. 137:2–4;
Dan. 6:18

Illustrative

- Of joy and gladness. . .Zeph. 3:17; Eph. 5:19
- Of heavenly felicity. . .Rev. 5:8–9
- (Ceasing of,) of calamities. . .Isa. 24:8–9;
Rev. 18:22

127. New Birth, The

The corruption of human nature requires. . .John 3:6;
Rom. 8:7–8

None can enter heaven without. . .John 3:3

Effected by

- God. . .John 1:13; 1 Pet. 1:3
- Christ. . .1 John 2:29
- The Holy Spirit. . .John 3:6; Titus 3:5

Is of the will of God. . .James 1:18

Is of the mercy of God. . .Titus 3:5

Is for the glory of God. . .Isa. 43:7

Described as

- A new creation. . .2 Cor. 5:17; Gal. 6:15; Eph. 2:10
- Newness of life. . .Rom. 6:4
- Putting on the new man. . .Eph. 4:24

128. Oaths

The lawful purpose of, explained. . .Heb. 6:16

Antiquity of. . .Gen. 14:22; 24:3, 8

Often accompanied by raising up the hand. . .Gen. 14:22; Dan. 12:7; Rev. 10:5–6

Often accompanied by placing the hand under the thigh of the person sworn to. . .Gen. 24:2, 9; 47:29

To be taken in fear and reverence. . .Eccles. 9:2

The Jews

- Forbidden to take, in name of idols. . .Josh. 23:7
- Forbidden to take in the name of any created thing. . .Matt. 5:34–36; James 5:12
- Forbidden to take false. . .Lev. 6:3; Zech. 8:17
- Forbidden to take rash, or unholy. . .Lev. 5:4
- Often guilty of rashly taking. . .Judg. 21:1, 7; Matt. 14:7–9; 26:72
- Often guilty of falsely taking. . .Lev. 6:3; Jer. 5:2; 7:9
- Condemned for false. . .Zech. 5:4; Mal. 3:5

- Condemned for profane. . .Jer. 23:10; Hosea 4:2

God used, to show the immutability of His counsel. . .
Gen. 22:16; Num. 14:28; Heb. 6:17

129. Obedience to God

Commanded. . .Deut. 13:4

Without faith, is impossible. . .Heb. 11:6

Better than sacrifice. . .1 Sam. 15:22

Justification obtained by that of Christ. . .Rom. 5:19

Christ, an example of. . .Matt. 3:15; John 15:20;
Phil. 2:5–8; Heb. 5:8

Angels engaged in. . .Ps. 103:20

A characteristic of saints. . .1 Pet. 1:14

Confess your failure in. . .Dan. 9:10

Prepare the heart for. . .1 Sam. 7:3; Ezra 7:10

Pray to be taught. . .Ps. 119:35; 143:10

Promises to. . .Exod. 23:22; 1 Sam. 12:14; Isa. 1:19;
Jer. 7:23

Blessedness of. . .Deut. 11:27; 28:1–13; Luke 11:28;
James 1:25

Punishment of refusing. . .Deut. 11:28; 28:15–68;
Josh. 5:6; Isa. 1:20

130. Offerings

To be made to God alone. . .Exod. 22:20; Judg. 13:16

Antiquity of. . .Gen. 4:3–4

Different kinds of

- Burnt. . .Lev. 1:3–17; Ps. 66:15
- Sin. . .Lev. 4:3–35; 6:25; 10:17
- Meat. . .Lev. 2:1–16; Num. 15:4
- Thank. . .Lev. 7:12; 22:29; Ps. 50:14
- Freewill. . .Lev. 23:38; Deut. 16:10; 23:23
- Incense. . .Exod. 30:8; Mal. 1:11; Luke 1:9
- First-fruits. . .Exod. 22:29; Deut. 18:4
- Tithe. . .Lev. 27:30; Num. 18:21; Deut. 14:22

Declared to be most holy. . .Num. 18:9

Unacceptable, without gratitude. . .Ps. 50:8, 14

131. Parables

Examples of

- Wise and foolish builders. . .Matt. 7:24–27
- New cloth and old garment. . .Matt. 9:16
- New wine and old bottles. . .Matt. 9:17
- Wicked husbandmen. . .Matt. 21:33–45
- Strong man armed. . .Mark 3:27; Luke 11:21
- Blind leading the blind. . .Luke 6:39
- Cloud and wind. . .Luke 12:54–57
- Barren fig tree. . .Luke 13:6–9
- Lost piece of silver. . .Luke 15:8–10

- Pharisee and Publican. . .Luke 18:9–14
- Talents. . .Luke 19:12–27
- Good Shepherd. . .John 10:1–6
- Vine and branches. . .John 15:1–5

132. Pardon

Promised. . .Isa. 1:18; Jer. 31:34; Heb. 8:12; Jer. 50:20

None without shedding of blood. . .Lev. 17:11;
Heb. 9:22

Sacrifices, ineffectual for. . .Heb. 10:4

Outward purifications, ineffectual for. . .Job 9:30–31;
Jer. 2:22

The blood of Christ, alone, is effective for. . .
Zech. 13:1; 1 John 1:7

Is granted

- By God alone. . .Dan. 9:9; Mark 2:7
- Through the blood of Christ. . .Matt. 26:28;
  Rom. 3:25; Col. 1:14
- According to the riches of grace. . .Eph. 1:7
- Abundantly. . .Isa. 55:7; Rom. 5:20
- All saints enjoy. . .Col. 2:13; 1 John 2:12

Blessedness of. . .Ps. 32:1; Rom. 4:7

133. Parents

Receive their children from God. . .Gen. 33:5;
1 Sam. 1:27; Ps. 127:3

Their duty to their children is

- To love them. . .Titus 2:4
- To bring them to Christ. . .Matt. 19:13–14
- To train them up for God. . .Prov. 22:6; Eph. 6:4
- To tell them of the miraculous works of God. . .
  Exod. 10:2; Ps. 78:4
- To command them to obey God. . .Deut. 32:46;
  1 Chron. 28:9
- To bless them. . .Gen. 48:15; Heb. 11:20
- To provide for them. . .Job 42:15; 2 Cor. 12:14;
  1 Tim. 5:8
- To rule them. . .1 Tim. 3:4, 12
- To correct them. . .
  Prov. 13:24; 19:18; 23:13; 29:17; Heb. 12:7
- Not to provoke them. . .Eph. 6:4; Col. 3:21

When faithful

- Are blessed by their children. . .Prov. 31:28
- Leave a blessing to their children. . .Ps. 112:2;
  Prov. 11:21; Isa. 65:23

134. Patience

God, is the God of. . .Rom. 15:5

Should have its perfect work. . .James 1:4

Trials of saints lead to. . .Rom. 5:3; James 1:3

Necessary to the inheritance of the promises. . .
   Heb. 6:12; 10:36

Exercise, toward all. . .1 Thess. 5:14

They who are in authority, should exercise. . .Matt. 18:26;
   Acts 26:3

Ministers should follow after. . .1 Tim. 6:11

Should be accompanied by
- Godliness. . .2 Pet. 1:6
- Faith. . .2 Thess. 1:4; Heb. 6:12; Rev. 13:10
- Temperance. . .2 Pet. 1:6
- Long-suffering. . .Col. 1:11
- Joyfulness. . .Col. 1:11

Saints strengthened to all. . .Col. 1:11

135. Peace

God is the author of. . .Ps. 147:14; Isa. 45:7;
   1 Cor. 14:33

Necessary to the enjoyment of life. . .Ps. 34:12, 14;
   1 Pet. 3:10–11

God bestows upon those who
- Obey Him. . .Lev. 26:3, 6
- Please Him. . .Ps. 16:7–8
- Endure His chastisement. . .Job 5:17, 23–24

Peace Offerings

Required to be perfect and free from blemish. . .
    Lev. 3:1, 6; 22:21

To be eaten before the Lord. . .Deut. 12:17–18

No unclean person to eat of. . .Lev. 7:20–21

Peace, Spiritual

God ordains. . .Isa. 26:12

The gospel is good tidings of. . .Rom. 10:15

Supports under trials. . .John 14:27; 16:33

136. Perfection

Is of God. . .Ps. 18:32; 138:8

All saints have, in Christ. . .1 Cor. 2:6; Phil. 3:15;
    Col. 2:10

God's perfection the standard of. . .Matt. 5:48

Implies

- Entire devotedness. . .Matt. 19:21
- Purity and holiness in speech. . .James 3:2

Saints commanded to aim at. . .Gen. 17:1; Deut. 18:13

Impossibility of attaining to. . .2 Chron. 6:36;
    Ps. 119:96

The Word of God is

- The rule of. . .James 1:25
- Designed to lead us to. . .2 Tim. 3:16–17

Love is the bond of. . .Col. 3:14

Patience leads to. . .James 1:4

Pray for. . .Heb. 13:20–21; 1 Pet. 5:10

137. Persecution

Christ suffered. . .Ps. 69:26; John 5:16

Christ voluntarily submitted to. . .Isa. 50:6

Christ was patient under. . .Isa. 53:7

Saints may expect. . .Mark 10:30; Luke 21:12; John 15:20

Saints suffer, for the sake of God. . .Jer. 15:15

Of saints, is a persecution of Christ. . .Zech. 2:8;
   Acts 9:4–5

All that live godly in Christ, shall suffer. . .2 Tim. 3:12

God doesn't forsake His saints under. . .2 Cor. 4:9

Cannot separate from Christ. . .Rom. 8:35. 37

Blessedness of enduring, for Christ's sake. . .Matt. 5:10;
   Luke 6:22

Pray for those suffering. . .2 Thess. 3:2

138. Perseverance

An evidence of reconciliation with God. . .Col. 1:21–23

An evidence of belonging to Christ. . .John 8:31;
   Heb. 3:6, 14

A characteristic of saints. . .Prov. 4:18

Promised to saints. . .Job 17:9

Leads to increase of knowledge. . .John 8:31–32

In well-doing
  • Leads to assurance of hope. . .Heb. 6:10–11
  • Is not in vain. . .1 Cor. 15:58; Gal. 6:9

Encouragement to. . .Heb. 12:2–3

Promises to. . .Matt. 10:22; 24:13; Rev. 2:26–28
Blessedness of. . .James 1:25

139. Poor, The

Made by God. . .Job 34:19; Prov. 22:2
Are such by God's appointment. . .1 Sam. 2:7; Job 1:21
God

- Regards equally with the rich. . .Job 34:19
- Protects. . .Ps. 12:5; 109:31

Christ lived as one of. . .Matt. 8:20
Christ preached to. . .Luke 4:18
Christ delivers. . .Ps. 72:12
Offerings of, acceptable to God. . .Mark 12:42–44;
    2 Cor. 8:2, 12
Don't rob. . .Prov. 22:22
Don't oppress. . .Deut. 24:14; Zech. 7:10
Don't despise. . .Prov. 14:21; James 2:2–4
Care for, illustrated. . .Luke 10:33–35

140. Power of Christ, The

As the Son of God, is the power of God. . .
    John 5:17–19; 10:28–30
As man, is from the Father. . .Acts 10:38
Shall be specially manifested at His second coming. . .
    Mark 13:26; 2 Pet. 1:16

Power of God, The

All things possible to. . .Matt. 19:26

Is the source of all strength. . .1 Chron. 29:12;
    Ps. 68:35

Works in, and for saints. . .2 Cor. 13:4; Eph. 1:19; 3:20

Exhibited in
- Creation. . .Gen. 1:2; Job 26:13; Ps. 104:30
- The conception of Christ. . .Luke 1:35
- Raising Christ from the dead. . .1 Pet. 3:18
- Working miracles. . .Rom. 15:19
- Overcoming all difficulties. . .Zech. 4:6–7

God's Word the instrument of. . .Eph. 6:17

141. *Praise*

God is worthy of. . .2 Sam. 22:4

Christ is worthy of. . .Rev. 5:12

God is glorified by. . .Ps. 22:23; 50:23

Is due to God on account of
- His majesty. . .Ps. 96:1, 6; Isa. 24:14
- His greatness. . .1 Chron. 16:25; Ps. 145:3
- His holiness. . .Exod. 15:11; Isa. 6:3
- His wisdom. . .Dan. 2:20; Jude 25
- His power. . .Ps. 21:13
- His goodness. . .Ps. 107:8; 118:1; 136:1; Jer. 33:11
- His mercy. . .2 Chron. 20:21;
        Ps. 89:1; 118:1–4; 136:1–26

Is a part of public worship. . .Ps. 9:14; 100:4; 118:19–20;
    Heb. 2:12

The heavenly host engage in. . .Isa. 6:2–3; Luke 2:13–14;
Rev. 4:9–11; 5:11–12

142. Prayer

<><><><><><><><><><><><><><><><><><><><><><><><><><><><>

Commanded. . .Isa. 55:6; Matt. 7:7; Phil. 4:6
God hears. . .Ps. 10:17; 65:2
God answers. . .Ps. 99:6; Isa. 58:9
Punishment for neglecting. . .Jer. 10:25

Prayer, Answers To
Of the righteous, avails much. . .James 5:16
Of the upright, a delight to God. . .Prov. 15:8
Granted
- Through the grace of God. . .Isa. 30:19
- Sometimes immediately. . .Isa. 65:24;
  Dan. 9:21, 23; 10:12
- Sometimes after delay. . .Luke 18:7
- Sometimes differently from our desire. . .
  2 Cor. 12:8–9
- Beyond expectation. . .Jer. 33:3; Eph. 3:20

Prayer, Private
Beneficial to the offerer. . .Job 42:10
Nothing should hinder. . .Dan. 6:10

Prayer, Public
Urge others to join in. . .Ps. 95:6; Zech. 8:21
Christ promises to be present at. . .Matt. 18:20

143. Pride

Is sin. . .Prov. 21:4

Hateful to God. . .Prov. 6:16–17; 16:5

Hateful to Christ. . .Prov. 8:12–13

Forbidden. . .1 Sam. 2:3; Rom. 12:3, 16

Defiles a man. . .Mark 7:20, 22

Hardens the mind. . .Dan. 5:20

A hindrance to seeking God. . .Ps. 10:4; Hosea 7:10

Comes from the heart. . .Mark 7:21–23

The wicked encompassed with. . .Ps. 73:6

Exhortation against. . .Jer. 13:15

144. Procrastination

Condemned by Christ. . .Luke 9:59–62

Saints avoid. . .Ps. 27:8; 119:60

To be avoided in

- Hearkening to God. . .Ps. 95:7–8; Heb. 3:7–8
- Seeking God. . .Isa. 55:6
- Glorifying God. . .Jer. 13:16
- Keeping God's commandments. . .Ps. 119:60
- Making offerings to God. . .Exod. 22:29
- Performance of vows. . .Deut. 23:21; Eccles. 5:4

Danger of, illustrated. . .Matt. 5:25; Luke 13:25

Exemplified

- Lot. . .Gen. 19:16
- Felix. . .Acts 24:25

145. Prophecies Respecting Christ

As the Son of God. . .Ps. 2:7
- Fulfilled. . .Luke 1:32, 35

As the seed of David. . .Ps. 132:11; Jer. 23:5
- Fulfilled. . .Acts 13:23; Rom. 1:3

His coming at a set time. . .Gen. 49:10; Dan. 9:24–25
- Fulfilled. . .Luke 2:1

His being anointed with the Spirit. . .Ps. 45:7;
Isa. 11:2; 61:1
- Fulfilled. . .Matt. 3:16; John 3:34; Acts 10:38

His ministry commencing in Galilee. . .Isa. 9:1–2
- Fulfilled. . .Matt. 4:12–16, 23

His hands and feet being nailed to the cross. . .Ps. 22:16
- Fulfilled. . .John 19:18; 20:25

His resurrection. . .Ps. 16:10; Isa. 26:19
- Fulfilled. . .Luke 24:6, 31, 34

146. Prophets

God spoke of old by. . .Hosea 12:10; Heb. 1:1

The messengers of God. . .2 Chron. 36:15; Isa. 44:26

The servants of God. . .Jer. 35:15

The watchmen of Israel. . .Ezek. 3:17

Were esteemed as holy men. . .2 Kings 4:9

Women sometimes endowed as. . .Joel 2:28

Were under the influence of the Holy Spirit while
prophesying. . .Luke 1:67; 2 Pet. 1:21

Prophets, False

Pretended to be sent by God. . .Jer. 23:17–18, 31

Not sent or commissioned by God. . .
   Jer. 14:14; 23:21; 29:31

Made use of by God to prove Israel. . .Deut. 13:3

Compared to wind. . .Jer. 5:13

Influenced by evil spirits. . .1 Kings 22:21–22

147. *Protection*

God is able to provide. . .1 Pet. 1:5; Jude 24

God is faithful to provide. . .1 Thess. 5:23–24;
   2 Thess. 3:3

Of God is
- Indispensable. . .Ps. 127:1
- Seasonable. . .Ps. 46:1
- Unfailing. . .Deut. 31:6; Josh. 1:5
- Effectual. . .John 10:28–30; 2 Cor. 12:9

Offered to
- Those who hearken to God. . .Prov. 1:33
- Returning sinners. . .Job 22:23, 25
- The perfect in heart. . .2 Chron. 16:9
- The poor. . .Ps. 14:6; 72:12–14
- The oppressed. . .Ps. 9:9
- The Church. . .Ps. 48:3; Zech. 2:4–5

148. Providence of God, The

Is His care over His works. . .Ps. 145:9

Is righteous. . .Ps. 145:17; Dan. 4:37

Is ever watchful. . .Ps. 121:4; Isa. 27:3

Is all-pervading. . .Ps. 139:1–5

All things are ordered by
- For His glory. . .Isa. 63:14
- For good to saints. . .Rom. 8:28

To be acknowledged
- In prosperity. . .Deut. 8:18; 1 Chron. 29:12
- In adversity. . .Job 1:21; Ps. 119:15
- In public calamities. . .Amos 3:6
- In all things. . .Prov. 3:6

Cannot be defeated. . .1 Kings 22:30, 34; Prov. 21:30

Result of depending upon. . .Luke 22:35

149. Punishment of the Wicked, The

Is from God. . .Lev. 26:18; Isa. 13:11

On account of their
- Sin. . .Lam. 3:39
- Iniquity. . .Jer. 36:31; Ezek. 3:17–18; 18:4, 13, 20; Amos 3:2
- Rejection of the law of God. . .1 Sam. 15:23; Hosea 4:6–9
- Disobeying God. . .Neh. 9:26–27; Eph. 5:6

In this life by

- Sickness. . .Lev. 26:16; Ps. 78:50
- Famine. . .Lev. 26:19–20, 26, 29; Ps. 107:34
- Fear. . .Lev. 26:36–37; Job 18:11
- Trouble and distress. . .Isa. 8:22; Zeph. 1:15

Consummated at the Day of Judgment. . .
Matt. 25:31, 46; Rom. 2:5, 16; 2 Pet. 2:9

150. Reaping

Is the cutting of the corn in harvest. . .Job 24:6

The sickle used for. . .Deut. 16:9; Mark 4:29

Both men and women engaged in. . .Ruth 2:8–9

The fields of others. . .Deut. 23:25

Mode of gathering the corn for, alluded to. . .Ps. 129:7;
Isa. 17:5

Grass after, was bound up into sheaves. . .Ps. 129:7

Persons engaged in

- Under the guidance of a steward. . .Ruth 2:5–6
- Visited by the master. . .Ruth 2:4; 2 Kings 4:18
- Fed by the master who himself presided at their
  meals. . .Ruth 2:14
- Received wages. . .John 4:36; James 5:4

A time of great rejoicing. . .Ps. 126:5–6

The Jews often hindered from, on account of their
sins. . .Mic. 6:15

Often unprofitable on account of sin. . .Jer. 12:13

151. Rebellion against God

Forbidden. . .Num. 14:9; Josh. 22:19

Provokes God. . .Num. 16:30; Neh. 9:26

Provokes Christ. . .Exod. 23:20–21; 1 Cor. 10:9

Vexes the Holy Spirit. . .Isa. 63:10

Connected with

- Stubbornness. . .Deut. 31:27
- Injustice and corruption. . .Isa. 1:20–23
- Contempt of God. . .Ps. 107:11

Man is prone to. . .Deut. 31:27; Rom. 7:14–18

The heart is the seat of. . .Jer. 5:23; Matt. 15:18–19;
    Heb. 3:12

Religious instruction designed to prevent. . .Ps. 78:5, 8

Promises to those who avoid. . .Deut. 28:1–13;
    1 Sam. 12:14

Forgiven upon repentance. . .Neh. 9:26–27

152. Reconciliation with God

Predicted. . .Dan. 9:24; Isa. 53:5

Proclaimed by angels at the birth of Christ. . .Luke 2:14

Effected for men

- By God in Christ. . .2 Cor. 5:19
- By Christ as High Priest. . .Heb. 2:17
- By the death of Christ. . .Rom. 5:10; Eph. 2:16;
    Col. 1:21–22
- By the blood of Christ. . .Eph. 2:13; Col. 1:20

Effects of
- Peace of God. . .Rom. 5:1; Eph. 2:16–17
- Access to God. . .Rom. 5:2; Eph. 2:18
- Union of Jews and Gentiles. . .Eph. 2:14
- Union of things in heaven and earth. . .
  Col. 1:20; Eph. 1:10

A pledge of final salvation. . .Rom. 5:10

Necessity for, illustrated. . .Matt. 5:24–26

153. Redemption

Defined. . .1 Cor. 6:20; 7:23

Is of God. . .Isa. 44:21–23; 43:1; Luke 1:68

Is by Christ. . .Matt. 20:28; Gal. 3:13

Is by the blood of Christ. . .Acts 20:28; Heb. 9:12;
   1 Pet. 1:19; Rev. 5:9

Christ sent to effect. . .Gal. 4:4–5

Christ is made, to us. . .1 Cor. 1:30

Man cannot effect. . .Ps. 49:7

Corruptible things cannot purchase. . .1 Pet. 1:18

The present life, the only season for. . .Job 36:18–19

A subject for praise. . .Isa. 44:22–23; 51:11

Old Testament saints partakers of. . .Heb. 9:15

154. Repentance

What it is. . .Isa. 45:22; Matt. 6:19–21; Acts 14:15;
2 Cor. 5:17; Col. 3:2; 1 Thess. 1:9; Heb. 12:1–2

Commanded to all by God. . .Ezek. 18:30–32;
Acts 17:30

Commanded by Christ. . .Rev. 2:5, 16; 3:3

Given by God. . .Acts 11:18; 2 Tim. 2:25

Christ came to call sinners to. . .Matt. 9:13

Christ exalted to give. . .Acts 5:31

By the operation of the Holy Spirit. . .Zech. 12:10

Called repentance to life. . .Acts 11:18

Called repentance to salvation. . .2 Cor. 7:10

Necessary to the pardon of sin. . .Acts 2:38; 3:19; 8:22

Conviction of sin necessary to. . .1 Kings 8:38;
Prov. 28:13; Acts 2:37–38; 19:18

There is joy in heaven over one sinner brought to. . .
Luke 15:7, 10

Should be evidenced by fruits. . .Isa. 1:16–17; Dan. 4:27;
Matt. 3:8; Acts 26:20

155. Resurrection

A doctrine of the Old Testament. . .Job 19:26;
Ps. 16:10; 49:15; Isa. 26:19; Dan. 12:2; Hosea 13:14

Expected by the Jews. . .John 11:24; Heb. 11:35

Denied by the Sadducees. . .Matt. 22:23; Luke 20:27;
Acts 23:8

Explained away by false teachers. . .2 Tim. 2:18

Called in question by some in the church. . .1 Cor. 15:12

Assumed and proved by our Lord. . .Matt. 22:29–32;
Luke 14:14; John 5:28–29

Preached by the apostles. . .Acts 4:2; 17:18; 24:15

Credibility of, shown by the resurrection of
individuals. . .Matt. 9:25; 27:53; Luke 7:14;
John 11:44; Heb. 11:35

Resurrection of Christ, The

Certainty of, proved by the resurrection of Christ. . .
1 Cor. 15:12–20

Foretold by the prophets. . .Ps. 16:10; Acts 13:34–35;
Isa. 26:19

Foretold by Himself. . .Matt. 20:19; Mark 9:9; 14:28;
John 2:19–22

A proof of His being the Son of God. . .Ps. 2:7;
Acts 13:33; Rom. 1:4

156. Revenge

<<<<<<<<<<<<<<<<<<<<<<<<<<<<<<<<<<<<<<<<<<<<<

Forbidden by our Lord. . .Lev. 19:18; Prov. 24:17, 29;
Matt. 5:39–41; Rom. 12:17, 19; 1 Thess. 5:15; 1 Pet. 3:9

Christ an example of restraint. . .Isa. 53:7; 1 Pet. 2:23

Rebuked by Christ. . .Luke 9:54–55

Inconsistent with Christian spirit. . .Luke 9:55

Proceeds from a spiteful heart. . .Ezek. 25:15

Instead of taking, we should
- Trust in God. . .Prov. 20:22; Rom. 12:16
- Exhibit love. . .Lev. 19:18; Luke 6:35
- Exercise restraint. . .Matt. 5:38–41
- Bless. . .Rom. 12:14
- Overcome others by kindness. . .Prov. 25:21–22; Rom. 12:20

Keep others from taking. . .1 Sam. 24:10; 25:24–31; 26:9
Be thankful for being kept from taking. . .1 Sam. 25:32–33
Punishment for. . .Ezek. 25:15–17; Amos 1:11–12

157. Reward of Saints, The

Is from God. . .Rom. 2:7; Col. 3:24; Heb. 11:6
Is of grace, through faith alone. . .Rom. 4:4–5, 16; 11:6
Is of God's good pleasure. . .Matt. 20:14–15; Luke 12:32
Prepared by God. . .Heb. 11:16
Prepared by Christ. . .John 14:2
Not on account of their merits. . .Rom. 4:4–5
Is great. . .Matt. 5:12; Luke 6:35; Heb. 10:35
Is full. . .2 John 8
Is sure. . .Prov. 11:18
Is satisfying. . .Ps. 17:15
Is inestimable. . .Isa. 64:4; 1 Cor. 2:9
Hope of, a cause of rejoicing. . .Rom. 5:2
Present afflictions not to be compared with. . .Rom. 8:18; 2 Cor. 5:17

Shall be given at the second coming of Christ. . .
  Matt. 16:27; Rev. 22:12

158. Riches

The true riches. . .Eph. 3:8; 1 Cor. 1:30; Col. 2:3;
  1 Pet. 2:7
God gives. . .1 Sam. 2:7; Eccles. 5:19
To God belongs this world's riches. . .Hag. 2:8
The blessing of the Lord brings. . .Prov. 10:22
Often an obstruction to the reception of the gospel. . .
  Mark 10:23–25
Deceitfulness of, chokes the Word. . .Matt. 13:22
The love of, the root of all evil. . .1 Tim. 6:10
Life doesn't consist in abundance of. . .Luke 12:15
Don't be overanxious for. . .Prov. 30:8
Don't strive for. . .Prov. 23:4
Cannot redeem the soul. . .Ps. 49:6–9; 1 Pet. 1:18
Heavenly treasures superior to. . .Matt. 6:19–20

159. Righteousness

Is obedience to God's law. . .Deut. 6:25; Rom. 10:5;
  Luke 1:6; Ps. 1:2
God loves. . .Ps. 11:7
God looks for. . .Isa. 5:7
None, by nature have. . .Job 15:14; Ps. 14:3; Rom. 3:10

No salvation by works of. . .Eph. 2:8–9; 2 Tim. 1:9;
Titus 3:5

Righteousness Imputed
Of saints endures forever. . .Ps. 112:3, 9; 2 Cor. 9:9
An evidence of the new birth. . .1 John 2:29

Righteousness of God, The
The kingdom of God is. . .Rom. 14:17
Christ is the end of the law for. . .Rom. 10:4
Christ called The Lord Our Righteousness. . .Jer. 23:6
The promises made through. . .Rom. 4:13
God delights in the exercise of. . .Jer. 9:24
The heavens shall declare. . .Ps. 50:6; 97:6

160. Sacrifices

Divine institution of. . .Gen. 3:21; 1:29; 9:3; 4:4–5;
Heb. 11:4
To be offered to God alone. . .Exod. 22:20;
Judg. 13:16; 2 Kings 17:36
When offered to God, an acknowledgment of His
being the supreme God. . .2 Kings 5:17; Jon. 1:16
Required to be perfect and without blemish. . .Lev. 22:19;
Deut. 15:21; 17:1; Mal. 1:8, 14
Generally the best of their kind. . .Gen. 4:4;
1 Sam. 15:22; Ps. 66:15; Isa. 1:11
To be brought to the place appointed by God. . .

Deut. 12:6; 2 Chron. 7:12

Were typical of Christ's sacrifice. . .1 Cor. 5:7; Eph. 5:2;
Heb. 10:1, 11–12

Were accepted when offered in sincerity and faith. . .
Gen. 4:4; Heb. 11:4; Gen. 8:21

Could not take away sin. . .Ps. 40:6; Heb. 9:9; 10:1–11

Without obedience, worthless. . .1 Sam. 15:22; Prov. 21:3;
Mark 12:33

The covenants of God confirmed by. . .Gen. 15:9–17;
Exod. 24:5–8; Heb. 9:19–20; Ps. 50:5

Offered to false gods, are offered to devils. . .Lev. 17:7;
Deut. 32:17; Ps. 106:37; 1 Cor. 10:20

161. Salvation

<<<<<<<<<<<<<<<<<<<<<<<<<<<<<<<<<<<<<<<<<<<<<

Is of God. . .Ps. 3:8; 37:39; Jer. 3:23

God is willing to give. . .1 Tim. 2:3–4

Is by Christ. . .Isa. 63:9; Eph. 5:23

Is not by works. . .Rom. 11:6; Eph. 2:9; 2 Tim. 1:9;
Titus 3:5

Is of grace. . .Eph. 2:5, 8; 2 Tim. 1:9; Titus 2:11

Is of love. . .Rom. 5:8; 1 John 4:9–10

Is of mercy. . .Ps. 6:4; Titus 3:5

Is of the long-suffering of God. . .2 Pet. 3:15

Is through faith in Christ. . .Mark 16:16; Acts 16:31;
Rom. 10:9; Eph.2:8; 1 Pet. 1:5

Reconciliation to God, a pledge of. . .Rom. 5:10

Confession of Christ necessary to. . .Rom. 10:10

The gospel is the power of God to. . .Rom. 1:16;
1 Cor. 1:18

The scriptures are able to make wise to. . .2 Tim. 3:15;
James 1:21

Now is the day of. . .Isa. 49:8; 2 Cor. 6:2

162. Sanctification

Is separation to the service of God. . .Ps. 4:3; 2 Cor. 6:17

In Christ. . .1 Cor. 1:2

Through the atonement of Christ. . .Heb. 10:10; 13:12

Through the Word of God. . .John 17:17, 19; Eph. 5:26

Christ made, of God, to us. . .1 Cor. 1:30

Saints elected to salvation through. . .2 Thess. 2:13;
1 Pet. 1:2

All saints are in a state of. . .Acts 20:32; 26:18;
1 Cor. 6:11

The Church made glorious by. . .Eph. 5:26–27

Offering up of saints acceptable through. . .Rom. 15:16

Saints fitted for the service of God by. . .2 Tim. 2:21

God wills all saints to have. . .1 Thess. 4:3

None can inherit the kingdom of God without. . .
1 Cor. 6:9–11

163. Scriptures, The

Given by inspiration of God. . .2 Tim. 3:16

Given by inspiration of the Holy Spirit. . .Acts 1:16;
2 Pet. 1:21

Contain the promises of the gospel. . .Rom. 1:2

Reveal the laws, statutes, and judgments of God. . .
Deut. 4:5, 14; Exod. 24:3–4

Record divine prophecies. . .2 Pet. 1:19–21

Testify of Christ. . .John 5:39; Acts 10:43; 18:28;
1 Cor. 15:3

Are full and sufficient. . .Luke 16:29, 31

Are an unerring guide. . .Prov. 6:23; 2 Pet. 1:19

Are able to make wise to salvation through faith in
Christ Jesus. . .2 Tim. 3:15

Are profitable both for doctrine and practice. . .
2 Tim. 3:16–17

Written for our instruction. . .Rom. 15:4

Intended for the use of all men. . .Rom. 16:26

Nothing to be taken from, or added to. . .Deut. 4:2; 12:32

One portion of, to be compared with another. . .
1 Cor. 2:13

164. *Second Coming of Christ, The*

◇◇◇◇◇◇◇◇◇◇◇◇◇◇◇◇◇◇◇◇◇◇◇◇◇◇◇◇◇◇◇◇◇◇

Time of, unknown. . .Matt. 24:36; Mark 13:32

Signs preceding. . .Matt. 24:3–51

The heavens and earth shall be dissolved. . .
2 Pet. 3:10, 12

They who shall have died in Christ will rise first at. . .
1 Thess. 4:16

The saints alive at, will be caught up to meet Him. . .
1 Thess. 4:17

Every eye shall see Him at. . .Rev. 1:7

Should be always considered as at hand. . .Rom. 13:12;
    Phil. 4:5; 1 Pet. 4:7
Blessedness of being prepared for. . .Matt. 24:46;
    Luke 12:37–38
The man of sin to be destroyed at. . .2 Thess. 2:8
Illustrated. . .Matt. 25:6; Luke 12:36, 39; 19:12, 15

165. Seeking God

Commanded. . .Isa. 55:6; Matt. 7:7
By prayer. . .Job 8:5; Dan. 9:3
In His house. . .Deut. 12:5; Ps. 27:4
Afflictions designed to lead to. . .Ps. 78:33–34;
    Hosea 5:15
Is never in vain. . .Isa. 45:19
Blessedness of. . .Ps. 119:2
Leads to joy. . .Ps. 70:4; 105:3
Ends in praise. . .Ps. 22:26
Promise connected with. . .Ps. 69:32
Shall be rewarded. . .Heb. 11:6
Punishment of those who neglect. . .Zeph. 1:4–6

166. Self-Denial

Christ set an example of. . .Matt. 4:8–10; 8:20;
    John 6:38; Rom. 15:3; Phil. 2:6–8
A test of devotedness to Christ. . .Matt. 10:37–38;
    Luke 9:23–24

Necessary

- In following Christ. . .Luke 14:27–33
- In the warfare of saints. . .2 Tim. 2:4
- To the triumph of saints. . .1 Cor. 9:25–27

Ministers especially called to exercise. . .2 Cor. 6:4–5

Suits strangers and pilgrims. . .Heb. 11:13–15; 1 Pet. 2:11

Danger of neglecting. . .Matt. 16:25–26; 1 Cor. 9:27

Reward of. . .Matt. 19:28–29; Rom. 8:13

Happy result. . .2 Pet. 1:4

167. Self-Examination

Directed. . .2 Cor. 13:5

Necessary before the communion. . .1 Cor. 11:28

Cause of difficulty in. . .Jer. 17:9

Should be engaged in

- With holy awe. . .Ps. 4:4
- With diligent search. . .Ps. 77:6; Lam. 3:40
- With prayer for divine searching. . .
  Ps. 26:2; 139:23–24
- With purpose of amendment. . .Ps. 119:59;
  Lam. 3:40

Advantages of. . .1 Cor. 11:31; Gal. 6:4; 1 John 3:20–22

168. Selfishness

Contrary to the law of God. . .Lev. 19:18; Matt. 22:39;
James 2:8

The example of Christ condemns. . .John 4:34;
Rom. 15:3; 2 Cor. 8:9

God hates. . .Mal. 1:10

Inconsistent with Christian love. . .1 Cor. 13:5

Inconsistent with communion of saints. . .
Rom. 12:4–5; 1 Cor. 12:12–27

Especially forbidden to saints. . .1 Cor. 10:24; Phil. 2:4

The love of Christ should constrain us to avoid. . .
2 Cor. 5:14–15

Ministers should be devoid of. . .1 Cor. 9:19–23; 10:33

All men addicted to. . .Eph. 2:3; Phil. 2:21

Saints falsely accused of. . .Job 1:9–11

Characteristic of the last days. . .2 Tim. 3:1–2

169. Self-Righteousness

Man is prone to. . .Prov. 20:6; 30:12

Hateful to God. . .Luke 16:15

Is boastful. . .Matt. 23:30

They who are given to

- Seek to justify themselves. . .Luke 10:29
- Reject the righteousness of God. . .Rom. 10:3
- Condemn others. . .Matt. 9:11–13; Luke 7:39
- Consider their own way right. . .Prov. 21:2

- Despise others. . .Isa. 65:5; Luke 18:9
- Proclaim their own goodness. . .Prov. 20:6
- Are pure in their own eyes. . .Prov. 30:12

Are abominable before God. . .Isa. 65:5

Saints renounce. . .Phil. 3:7–10

Warning against. . .Deut. 9:4

170. Self-Will and Stubbornness

Forbidden. . .2 Chron. 30:8; Ps. 75:5; 95:8

Proceed from
- Unbelief. . .2 Kings 17:14
- Pride. . .Neh. 9:16, 29
- An evil heart. . .Jer. 7:24

God knows. . .Isa. 48:4

Heinousness of. . .1 Sam. 15:23

Characteristic of the wicked. . .Prov. 7:11; 2 Pet. 2:10

The wicked do not cease from. . .Judg. 2:19

Punishment for. . .Deut. 21:20–21; Prov. 29:1

Illustrated. . .Ps. 32:9; Jer. 31:18

171. Sickness

Sent by God. . .Deut. 28:59–61; 32:39; 2 Sam. 12:15;
Acts 12:23

The devil sometimes permitted to inflict. . .Job 2:6–7;
Luke 9:39; 13:16

Often brought on by intemperance. . .Hosea 7:5

Often sent as a punishment of sin. . .Lev. 26:14–16;
2 Chron. 21:12–15; 1 Cor. 11:29–30

Healing of, lawful on the Sabbath. . .Luke 13:14–16

Christ compassionate toward those in. . .Isa. 53:4;
Matt. 8:16–17

Faith required in those healed of, by Christ. . .
Matt. 9:28–29; Mark 5:34; 10:52

Often incurable by human means. . .Deut. 28:27;
2 Chron. 21:18

Visiting those in, an evidence of belonging to Christ. . .
Matt. 25:34, 36, 40

Pray for those afflicted with. . .Acts 28:8;
James 5:14–15

God's aid should be sought in. . .2 Chron. 16:12

172. Simplicity

Is opposed to fleshly wisdom. . .2 Cor. 1:12

Necessity for. . .Matt. 18:2–3

Exhortation to. . .Rom. 16:19; 1 Pet. 2:2

They who have the grace of

- Are made wise by God. . .Matt. 11:25
- Are made wise by the Word of God. . .
  Ps. 19:7; 119:130
- Are preserved by God. . .Ps. 116:6
- Made circumspect by instruction. . .Prov. 1:4
- Profit by the correction of others. . .
  Prov. 19:25; 21:11

Beware of being corrupted from that, which is in
   Christ. . .2 Cor. 11:3
Illustrated. . .Matt. 6:22

173. Sin

Is the transgression of the law. . .1 John 3:4
Is of the devil. . .1 John 3:8; John 8:44
All unrighteousness is. . .1 John 5:17
Whatever is not of faith is. . .Rom. 14:23
The thought of foolishness is. . .Prov. 24:9
Entered into the world by Adam. . .Gen. 3:6–7;
   Rom. 5:12
All men are conceived and born in. . .Gen. 5:3;
   Job 15:14; 25:4; Ps. 51:5
All men are shaped in. . .Ps. 51:5
Scripture concludes all under. . .Gal. 3:22
No man is without. . .1 Kings 8:46; Eccles. 7:20
Christ alone was without. . .2 Cor. 5:21; Heb. 4:15; 7:26;
   1 John 3:5
No man can cleanse himself from. . .Job 9:30–31;
   Prov. 20:9; Jer. 2:22
Christ was manifested to take away. . .John 1:29;
   1 John 3:5
Christ's blood cleanses from. . .1 John 1:7

174. Sobriety

Commanded. . .1 Pet. 1:13; 5:8

The gospel designed to teach. . .Titus 2:11–12

With watchfulness. . .1 Thess. 5:6

With prayer. . .1 Pet. 4:7

Required in

- Ministers. . .1 Tim. 3:2–3; Titus 1:8
- Wives of ministers. . .1 Tim. 3:11
- Aged men. . .Titus 2:2
- Young men. . .Titus 2:6
- Young women. . .Titus 2:4
- All saints. . .1 Thess. 5:6, 8

Women should exhibit, in dress. . .1 Tim. 2:9

We should estimate our character and talents with. . .
Rom. 12:3

We should live in. . .Titus 2:12

Motives to. . .1 Pet. 4:7; 5:8

175. Temptation

Does not come from God. . James 1:13

The devil is the author of. . .1 Chron. 21:1; Matt. 4:1;
John 13:2; 1 Thess. 3:5

Evil associates, the instruments of. . .
Prov. 1:10; 7:6, 10, 25; 16:29

Always conformable to the nature of man. . .1 Cor. 10:13

Often ends in sin and destruction. . .1 Tim. 6:9;
James 1:15

God will not suffer saints to be exposed to, beyond
    their powers to bear. . .1 Cor. 10:13
God will make a way for saints to escape out of. . .
    1 Cor. 10:13
God enables the saints to bear. . .1 Cor. 10:13
God knows how to deliver saints out of. . .2 Pet. 2:9
Christ keeps faithful saints from the hour of. . .
    Rev. 3:10
Saints may be in heaviness through. . .1 Pet. 1:6
Blessedness of those who meet and overcome. . .
    James 1:2–4, 12

176. Thanksgiving

Christ set an example of. . .Matt. 11:25; 26:27;
    John 6:11; 11:41
The heavenly host engaged in. . .
    Rev. 4:9; 7:11–12; 11:16–17
Commanded. . .Ps. 50:14; Phil. 4:6
Is a good thing. . .Ps. 92:1
Should be offered
  • In the name of Christ. . .Eph. 5:20
  • Before taking food. . John 6:11; Acts 27:35
  • For victory over death and the grave. . .
    1 Cor. 15:57
  • For the nearness of God's presence. . .Ps. 75:1
  • For the supply of our bodily wants . . .Rom. 14:6–7;
    1 Tim. 4:3–4

Should be accompanied by intercession for others. . .
1 Tim. 2:1; 2 Tim. 1:3; Philem. 1:4

Should always accompany prayer. . .Neh. 11:17;
Phil. 4:6; Col. 4:2

Should always accompany praise. . .Ps. 92:1; Heb. 13:15

Expressed in psalms. . .1 Chron. 16:7

177. Theft

Is an abomination. . .Jer. 7:9–10

Forbidden. . .Exod. 20:15; Mark 10:19; Rom. 13:9

From the poor specially forbidden. . .Prov. 22:22–23

Includes fraud in general. . .Lev. 19:13

Includes fraud concerning wages. . .Lev. 19:13; Mal. 3:5;
James 5:4

Proceeds from the heart. . .Matt. 15:19

Defiles a man. . .Matt. 15:19–20

Connected with murder. . .Jer. 7:9; Hosea 4:2

Shame follows the detection of. . .Jer. 2:26

Brings a curse on those who commit it. . .Hosea 4:2–3;
Zech. 5:3–4; Mal. 3:5

Brings the wrath of God upon those who commit it. . .
Ezek. 22:29, 31

Heavenly treasure secure from. . .Matt. 6:20; Luke 12:33

178. Time

The duration of the world. . .Job 22:16; Rev. 10:6

The measure of the continuance of anything. . .
   Judg. 18:31

An appointed season. . .Neh. 2:6; Eccles. 3:1, 17

Computed by
   * Years. . .Gen. 15:13; 2 Sam. 21:1; Dan. 9:2
   * Months. . .Num. 10:10; 1 Chron. 27:1; Job 3:6
   * Weeks. . .Dan. 10:2; Luke 18:12
   * Days. . .Gen. 8:3; Job 1:4; Luke 11:3
   * Hours, after the captivity. . .Dan. 5:5; John 11:9
   * Moments. . .Exod. 33:5; Luke 4:5; 1 Cor. 15:52

Shortness of man's portion of. . .Ps. 89:47

Should be spent in fear of God. . .1 Pet. 1:17

All events of, predetermined by God. . .Acts 17:26

All God's purposes fulfilled in due time. . .Mark 1:15;
   Gal. 4:4

179. Tithe

The tenth of anything. . .1 Sam. 8:15, 17

Considered a just return to God for His blessings. . .
   Gen. 28:22

Under the law belonged to God. . .Lev. 27:30

Consisted of a tenth
   * Of all the produce of the land. . .Lev. 27:30
   * Of all cattle. . .Lev. 27:32

- Of holy things dedicated. . .2 Chron. 31:6

Given by God to the Levites for their services. . .
   Num. 18:21, 24; Neh. 10:37

Punishment for changing. . .Lev. 27:32–33

The Jews slow in giving. . .Neh. 13:10–12

The Jews reproved for withholding. . .Mal. 3:8

180. Titles and Names of Christ

Examples of
- Amen. . .Rev. 3:14
- Alpha and Omega. . .Rev. 1:8; 22:13
- Arm of the Lord. . .Isa. 51:9; 53:1
- Branch. . .Jer. 23:5; Zech. 3:8; 6:12
- Counselor. . .Isa. 9:6
- Door. . .John 10:7
- Dayspring. . .Luke 1:78
- Elect of God. . .Isa. 42:1
- Forerunner. . .Heb. 6:20
- Prince of life. . .Acts 3:15
- Shiloh. . .Gen. 49:10
- True Vine. . .John 15:1
- Witness. . .Isa. 55:4
- Wonderful. . .Isa. 9:6

181. Titles and Names of the Devil

Examples of
- Adversary. . .1 Pet. 5:8
- Dragon. . .Isa. 27:1; Rev. 20:2
- Enemy. . .Matt. 13:39
- Father of lies. . .John 8:44
- Lying spirit. . .1 Kings 22:22
- Murderer. . .John 8:44
- Power of darkness. . .Col. 1:13
- Prince of this world. . .John 14:30
- Ruler of the darkness of this world. . .Eph. 6:12
- Satan. . .1 Chron. 21:1; Job 1:6
- Tempter. . .Matt. 4:3; 1 Thess. 3:5
- The god of this world. . .2 Cor. 4:4

182. Titles and Names of the Holy Spirit

Examples of
- Breath of the Almighty. . .Job 33:4
- Comforter. . .John 14:16, 26; 15:26
- Power of the Highest. . .Luke 1:35
- Spirit of the Lord. . .Isa. 11:2; Acts 5:9
- Spirit of God. . .Gen. 1:2; 1 Cor. 2:11; Job 33:4
- Spirit of adoption. . .Rom. 8:15
- Spirit of wisdom. . .Isa. 11:2; Eph. 1:17
- Spirit of counsel. . .Isa. 11:2
- Spirit of might. . .Isa. 11:2

- Spirit of truth. . John 14:17; 15:26
- Spirit of holiness. . .Rom. 1:4
- Spirit of revelation. . .Eph. 1:17

183. *Truth*

Christ is. . .John 14:6; 7:18
The Holy Spirit is the Spirit of. . John 14:17
God regards, with favor. . Jer. 5:3
The judgments of God are according to. . .
    Ps. 96:13; Rom. 2:2
Is part of Christian armor. . .Eph. 6:14

Truth of God, The
Should be obeyed. . .Rom. 2:8; Gal. 3:1
Should be loved. . .2 Thess. 2:10
Should be rightly divided. . .2 Tim. 2:15
Remembered toward saints. . .Ps. 98:3
Is a shield and buckler to saints. . .Ps. 91:4
Is denied by

- The devil. . .Gen. 3:4–5
- The self-righteous. . .1 John 1:10
- Unbelievers. . .1 John 5:10

184. Types of Christ

Examples of

- Adam. . .Rom. 5:14; 1 Cor. 15:45
- Ark of the Covenant. . .Exod. 25:16; Ps. 40:8; Isa. 42:6
- Burnt offering. . .Lev. 1:2, 4; Heb. 10:10
- Cities of refuge. . .Num. 35:6; Heb. 6:18
- David. . .2 Sam. 8:15; Ezek. 37:24; Ps. 89:19–20
- First-fruits. . .Exod. 22:29; 1 Cor. 15:20
- Isaac. . .Gen. 22:1–2; Heb. 11:17–19
- Passover lamb. . .Exod. 12:3–6, 46; John 19:36; 1 Cor. 5:7
- Peace offerings. . .Lev. 3:1; Eph. 2:14, 16
- Scapegoat. . .Lev. 16:20–22; Isa. 53:12
- Sin offering. . .Lev. 4:2–3, 12; Heb. 13:11–12
- Temple. . .1 Kings 6:1, 38; John 2:19, 21
- Tree of life. . .Gen. 2:9; Rev. 22:2

185. Unbelief

Is sin. . .John 16:9

Defilement inseparable from. . .Titus 1:15

Rebuked by Christ. . .Matt. 17:17; John 20:27

Was an impediment to the performance of miracles. . . Matt. 17:20; Mark 6:5–6

Miracles designed to convince those in. . .John 10:37–38; 1 Cor. 14:22

The Jews rejected for. . .Rom. 11:7, 20

Believers should hold no communion with those in. . .
2 Cor. 6:14

Warnings against. . .Heb. 3:12; 4:11

Pray for help against. . .Mark 9:24

The portion of, awarded to all unfaithful servants. . .
Luke 12:46

186. Union with Christ

As Head of the church. . .Eph. 1:20, 22–23; 4:15–16;
Col. 1:18

Christ prayed that all saints might have. . .John 17:21, 23

Includes union with the Father. . .John 17:21; 1 John 2:24

Is of God. . .1 Cor. 1:30

The Holy Spirit witnesses. . .1 John 3:24

The gift of the Holy Spirit is an evidence of. . .
1 John 4:13

Necessary to growth in grace. . .Eph. 4:15–16; Col. 2:19

Necessary to fruitfulness. . .John 15:4–5

They who have, ought to walk as He walked. . .
1 John 2:6

False teachers have not. . .Col. 2:18–19

Is indissoluble. . .Rom. 8:35

Punishment of those who lack. . .John 15:6

187. Uprightness

God is perfect in. . .Isa. 26:7

God has pleasure in. . .1 Chron. 29:17

God created man in. . .Eccles. 7:29

Man has deviated from. . .Eccles. 7:29

Being kept from presumptuous sins is necessary to. . .
  Ps. 19:13

With poverty, is better than sin with riches. . .Prov. 28:6

With poverty, is better than folly. . .Prov. 19:1

The truly wise walk in. . .Prov. 15:21

The way of, is to depart from evil. . .Prov. 16:17

A characteristic of saints. . .Ps. 111:1; Isa. 26:7

Saints should resolve to walk in. . .Ps. 26:11

Pray for those who walk in. . .Ps. 125:4

Reprove those who deviate from. . .Gal. 2:14

188. Vanity

A consequence of the fall. . .Rom. 8:20

The thoughts of man are. . .Ps. 94:11

The days of man are. . .Job 7:16; Eccles. 6:12

Childhood and youth are. . .Eccles. 11:10

The beauty of man is. . .Ps. 39:11; Prov. 31:30

Worldly wisdom is. . .Eccles. 2:15, 21; 1 Cor. 3:19–20

Worldly pleasure is. . .Eccles. 2:1

Worldly anxiety is. . .Ps. 39:6; 127:2

Worldly labor is. . .Eccles. 2:11; 4:4

Worldly enjoyment is. . .Eccles. 2:3, 10–11

Worldly possessions are. . .Eccles. 2:4–11

Fools follow those given to. . .Prov. 12:11

Following those given to, leads to poverty. . .Prov. 28:19

189. Vines

Often found wild. . .2 Kings 4:39; Hosea 9:10

Required to be dressed and pruned to increase its
fruitfulness. . .Lev. 25:3; 2 Chron. 26:10; Isa. 18:5

The dwarf and spreading vine particularly esteemed. . .
Ezek. 17:6

Often degenerated. . .Isa. 5:2; Jer. 2:21

Frequently injured by hail and frost. . .Ps. 78:47; 105:32–33

Foxes destructive to. . .Song of Sol. 2:15

Young cattle fed on its leaves and tender shoots. . .
Gen. 49:11

Perfumed the air with the fragrance of its flowers. . .
Song of Sol. 2:13; Hosea 14:7

God made, fruitful for His people when obedient. . .
Joel 2:22; Zech. 8:12

Frequently made unfruitful as a punishment. . .Jer. 8:13;
Hosea 2:12; Joel 1:7, 12; Hag. 2:19

Nazarites prohibited eating any part of. . .Num. 6:2–4

190. Vows

Solemn promises made to God. . .Ps. 76:11

Were made in reference to

- Devoting the person to God. . .Num. 6:2
- Dedicating children to God. . .1 Sam. 1:11
- Devoting property to God. . .Gen. 28:22
- Offering sacrifices. . .Lev. 7:16; 22:18–22;
  Num. 15:3

To be voluntary. . .Deut. 23:21–22

To be performed faithfully. . .Num. 30:2

To be performed without delay. . .Deut. 23:21, 23

Danger of inconsiderately making. . .Prov. 20:25

191. Waiting upon God

As the God of providence. . .Jer. 14:22

As the God of salvation. . .Ps. 25:5

As the giver of all temporal blessings. . .Ps. 104:27–28;
  Ps. 145:15–16

Is good. . .Ps. 52:9

God calls us to. . .Zeph. 3:8

Exhortations and encouragements to. . .Ps. 27:14; 37:7;
  Hosea 12:6

Saints plead, in prayer. . .Ps. 25:21; Isa. 33:2

The patience of saints often tried in. . .Ps. 69:3

Exemplified

- Jacob. . .Gen. 49:1, 18
- Hannah. . .1 Sam. 1:2, 7, 20
- David. . .Ps. 39:7

192. Warfare of Saints

Is not after the flesh. . .2 Cor. 10:3

Is a good warfare. . .1 Tim. 1:18–19

Called the good fight of faith. . .1 Tim. 6:12

Is against

- The devil. . .Gen. 3:15; 2 Cor. 2:11; Eph. 6:12;
  James 4:7; 1 Pet. 5:8; Rev. 12:17
- The flesh. . .Rom. 7:23; 1 Cor. 9:25–27;
  2 Cor. 12:7; Gal. 5:17; 1 Pet. 2:11
- Enemies. . .Ps. 38:19; 56:2; 59:3
- The world. . .John 16:33; 1 John 5:4–5
- Death. . .1 Cor. 15:26; Heb. 2:14–15

Often arises from the opposition of friends or relatives. . .
Mic. 7:6; Matt. 10:35–36

Illustrated. . .Isa. 9:5; Zech. 10:5

193. Watchfulness

Christ an example of. . .Matt. 26:38, 40; Luke 6:12

Commanded. . .Mark 13:37; Rev. 3:2

Exhortations to. . .1 Thess. 5:6; 1 Pet. 4:7

God especially requires in ministers. . .Ezek. 3:17;
Isa. 62:6; Mark 13:34

Ministers exhorted to. . .Acts 20:31; 2 Tim. 4:5

Faithful ministers exercise. . .Heb. 13:17

Faithful ministers approved by. . .Matt. 24:45–46;
Luke 12:41–44

Saints pray to be kept in a state of. . .Ps. 141:3

Blessedness of. . .Luke 12:37; Rev. 16:15

Danger of remissness in. . .Matt. 24:48–51; 25:5, 8, 12;
Rev. 3:3

Illustrated. . .Luke 12:35–36

194. Wicked, Compared To

Abominable branches. . .Isa. 14:19

Ashes under the feet. . .Mal. 4:3

Bad fishes. . .Matt. 13:47–48

Clouds without water. . .Jude 12

Dogs. . .Prov. 26:11; Matt. 7:6; 2 Pet. 2:22

Green herbs. . .Ps. 37:2

Melting wax. . .Ps. 68:2

Wandering stars. . .Jude 13

Wayward children. . .Matt. 11:16

Wells without water. . .2 Pet. 2:17

195. Wine

First mention of. . .Gen. 9:20–21

Was made of

• The juice of the grape. . .Gen. 49:11

• The juice of the pomegranate. . .Song of Sol. 8:2

Generally made by treading the grapes in a press. . .
Neh. 13:15; Isa. 63:2–3

Many kinds of. . .Neh. 5:18

Sweet, esteemed for flavor and strength. . .Isa. 49:26;
Amos 9:13; Mic. 6:15

Red, most esteemed. . .Prov. 23:31; Isa. 27:2

Often spiced to increase its strength. . .Prov. 9:2, 5; 23:30

First fruits of, to be offered to God. . .Deut. 18:4;
2 Chron. 31:5

Consequence of putting (when new), into old bottles. . .
Mark 2:22

196. Wisdom of God, The

Described as
- Perfect. . .Job 36:4; 37:16
- Mighty. . .Job 36:5
- Universal. . .Job 28:24; Dan. 2:22; Acts 15:18
- Infinite. . .Ps. 147:5; Rom. 11:33
- Unsearchable. . .Isa. 40:28; Rom. 11:33
- Wonderful. . .Ps. 139:6
- Beyond human comprehension. . .Ps. 139:6
- Incomparable. . .Isa. 44:6–7; Jer. 10:7
- Underived. . .Job 21:22; Isa. 40:14

The gospel contains treasures of. . .1 Cor. 2:7

All human wisdom derived from. . .Dan. 2:21

Nothing is concealed from. . .Ps. 139:12

Not to be selected from among the ungodly. . .
   Gen. 24:3; 26:34–35; 28:1

Duties of, to their husbands
   • To love them. . .Titus 2:4
   • To reverence them. . .Eph. 5:33
   • To be faithful to them. . .1 Cor. 7:3–5, 10
   • To be subject to them. . .Gen. 3:16; Eph. 5:22, 24;
     1 Pet. 3:1
   • To obey them. . .1 Cor. 14:34; Titus 2:5
   • To remain with them for life. . .Rom. 7:2–3

Should be adorned
   • Not with ornaments. . .1 Tim. 2:9; 1 Pet. 3:3
   • With modesty and sobriety. . .1 Tim. 2:9
   • With a meek and quiet spirit. . .1 Pet. 3:4–5
   • With good works. . .1 Tim. 2:10; 5:10

Should seek religious instruction from their husbands. . .
   1 Cor. 14:35

198. Works, Good

Christ, an example of. . .John 10:32; Acts 10:38

Called

- Good fruits. . .James 3:17
- Fruits meet for repentance. . .Matt. 3:8
- Fruits of righteousness. . .Phil. 1:11
- Works and labors of love. . .Heb. 6:10

Are by Jesus Christ to the glory and praise of God. . .
Phil. 1:11

They alone, who abide in Christ can perform. . .
John 15:4–5

Wrought by God in us. . .Isa. 26:12; Phil. 2:13

The scripture designed to lead us to. . .2 Tim. 3:16–17;
James 1:25

To be performed in Christ's name. . .Col. 3:17

Heavenly wisdom is full of. . .James 3:17

Justification unattainable by. . .Rom. 3:20; Gal. 2:16

Salvation unattainable by. . .Eph. 2:8–9; 2 Tim. 1:9;
Titus 3:5

God remembers. . .Neh. 13:14; Heb. 6:9–10

God is glorified by. . .John 15:8

199. Zeal

Christ an example of. . .Ps. 69:9; John 2:17

Godly sorrow leads to. . .2 Cor. 7:10–11

Of saints, ardent. . .Ps. 119:139

Provokes others to do good. . .2 Cor. 9:2

Should be exhibited

- In spirit. . .Rom. 12:11
- In well-doing. . .Gal. 4:18; Titus 2:14
- In desiring the salvation of others. . .Acts 26:29; Rom. 10:1
- In contending for the faith. . .Jude 3
- In missionary labors. . .Rom. 15:19, 23
- For the glory of God. . .Num. 25:11, 13
- For the welfare of saints. . .Col. 4:13
- Against idolatry. . .2 Kings 23:4–14

Sometimes wrongly directed. . .2 Sam. 21:2; Acts 22:3–4; Phil. 3:6

Sometimes not according to knowledge. . .Rom. 10:2; Gal. 1:14; Acts 21:20

Ungodly men sometimes pretend to. . .2 Kings 10:16; Matt. 23:15

Exhortation to. . .Rom. 12:11; Rev. 3:19

Notes

If you enjoyed

Explore Your Bible

be sure to look for these other great Bible
resources from Barbour Publishing!

The Complete Guide to the Bible
7" x 9½", paperback, 528 pages
ISBN 978-1-59789-374-9

*500 Questions & Answers from
the Bible*
6" x 9", paperback, 256 pages
ISBN 978-1-59789-473-9

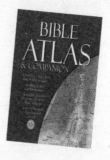

Bible Atlas & Companion
8" x 10", paperback, 176 pages
ISBN 978-1-59789-779-2

Available wherever Christian books are sold.